24 Key Pieces of the Girona Art Museum

md'A Museu d'Art de Girona
Generalitat de Catalunya Departament de Cultura
Bisbat de Girona
Diputació de Girona

Visitor's Guide
by Narcís-Jordi Aragó

24 Key Pieces of the Girona Art Museum

md'A Museu d'Art de Girona

A Museum in a Palace

The Museu d'Art in Girona is housed in one of the city's noblest buildings: the Episcopal Palace, which is more than a thousand years old. The Romanesque and Gothic parts were enlarged in the Renaissance period and completed during the nineteenth century until taking on the current structure.

The Palace is decorated with the coats of arms of the successive prelates who lived there from its construction until 1973, when Bishop Jaume Camprodon rejected it to live in a rented flat. During the 1936-1939 Spanish Civil War, and in the absence of Bishop Josep Cartañà, the idea emerged of setting up a People's Museum, the first premonition of its current use.

For many years the building was also the headquarters of the Ecclesiastical Court and the prison for holding clergymen on trial. The kings also regularly stayed in its rooms during their visits to the city. There are still clearly visible remains of this past: the prison enclosure, the baroque Episcopal chapel, gravestones with inscriptions, heraldic seals and the coat of arms of Emperor Charles V in the Throne Room.

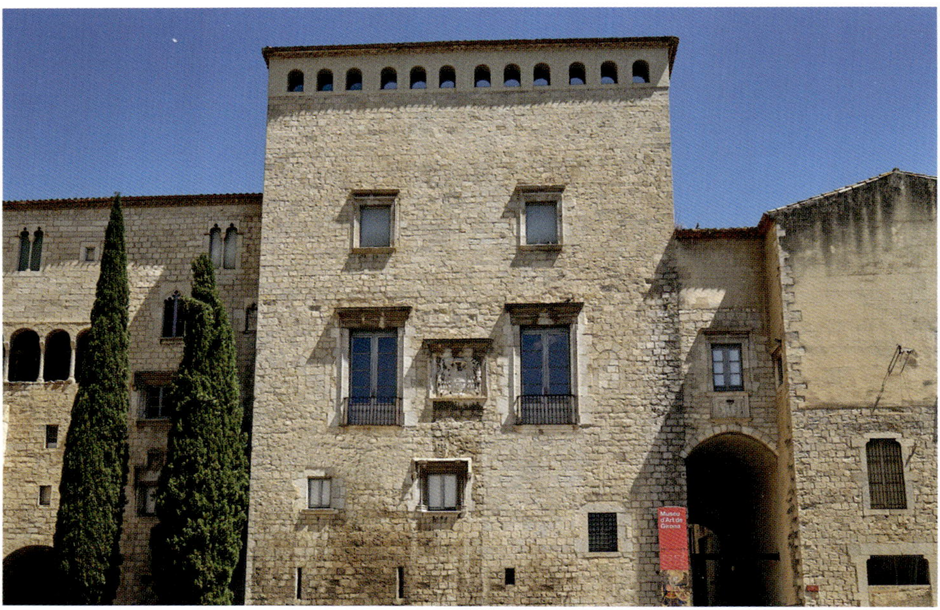

Sixteen centuries of Girona art

The works exhibited at the Episcopal Palace are basically from the former Diocesan Museum and the Provincial Museum of Antiquities and Fine Arts, as well as the Girona Provincial Council Art Collection.

The visit to the building allows you to see, in chronological order, a complete panorama of Girona art over sixteen centuries through pictorial and sculptural pieces from successive periods and styles: Romanesque, Gothic, Renaissance, baroque, realism, Catalan art nouveau and *Noucentisme*. There are also themed rooms on ceramics, glassware and the art of the Catholic liturgy, as well as areas for temporary shows and contemporary art exhibitions. Its many windows frame landscapes comparable to the works of art it holds: views over the cathedral, the Museum gardens and the city of Girona.

Of the approximately 500 works on display in the Museum, we have chosen **twenty-four**, which are considered particularly significant for their characteristics or essential due to their exceptional nature. Through these and others, you can trace the artistic life and social history of the city and Catalonia.

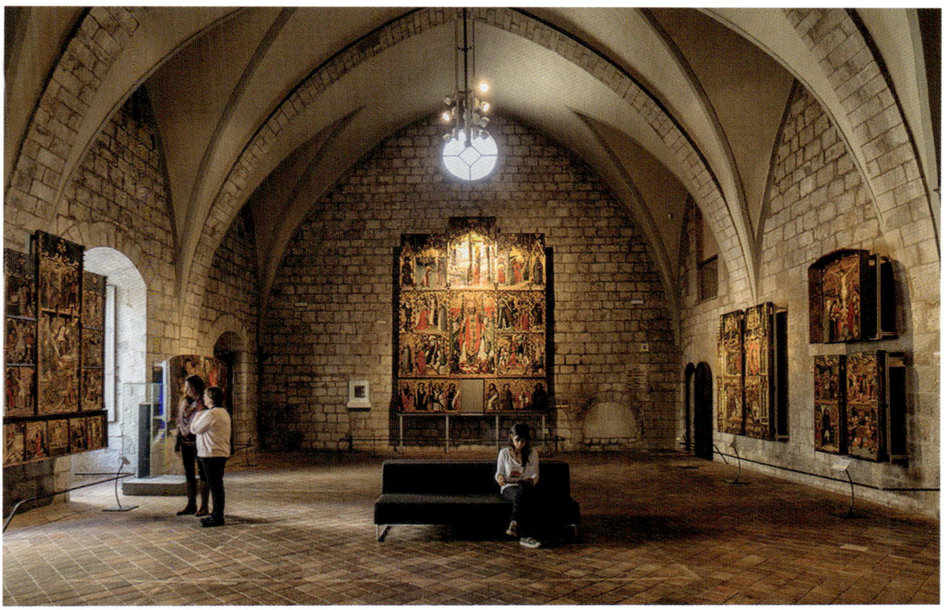

CONTENTS

Selection of works

PRE-ROMANESQUE & ROMANESQUE

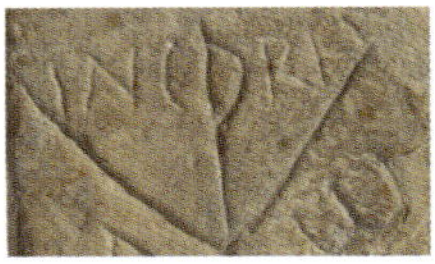

1. Fragment of an early Christian gravestone
p. 10

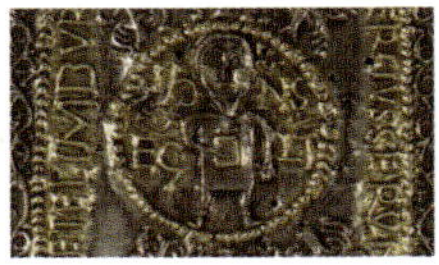

2. Portable altar of Sant Pere de Rodes
p. 12

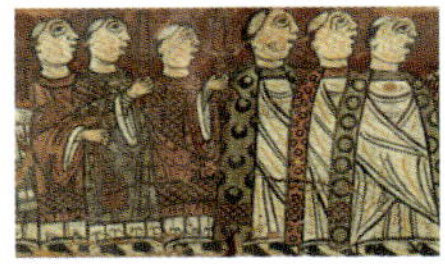

3. Cruïlles beam
p. 14

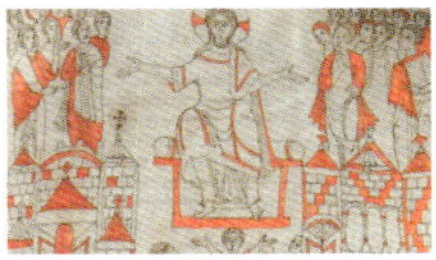

4. *Bede's Book of Homilies*
p. 16

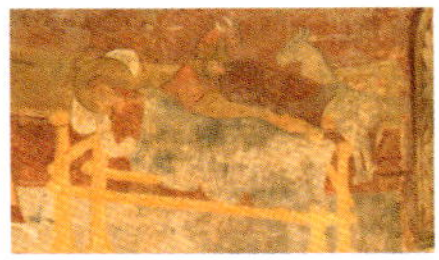

5. Apse of Pedrinyà
p. 18

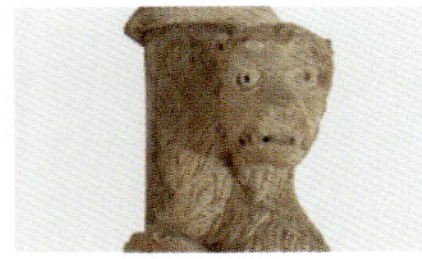

6. *The Lioness*
p. 20

GOTHIC

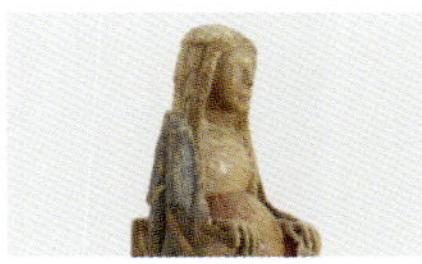

7. *Our Lady of Hope*
p. 22

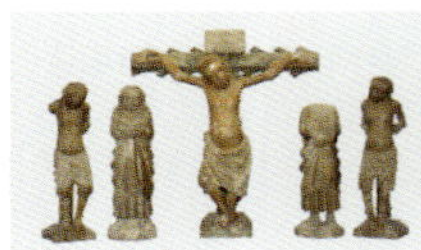

8. *Calvary*
p. 24

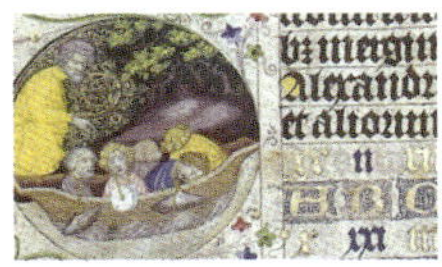

9. *Usuard's Martyrology*
p. 26

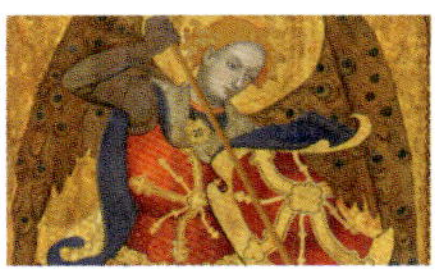

10. Altarpiece of Sant Miquel de Cruïlles
p. 28

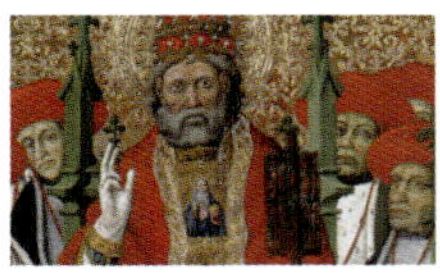

11. Altarpiece of Sant Pere de Púbol
p. 30

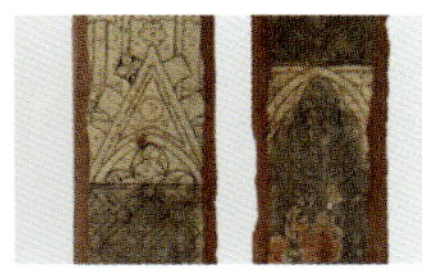

13. Stained glassmaker's work tables
p. 34

RENAISSANCE

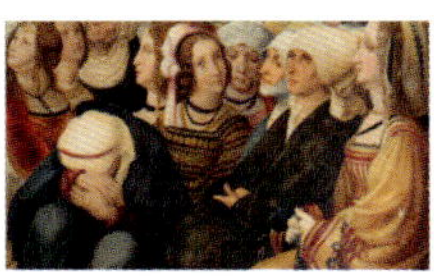

12. *Preaching of Saint Felix in Girona*
p. 32

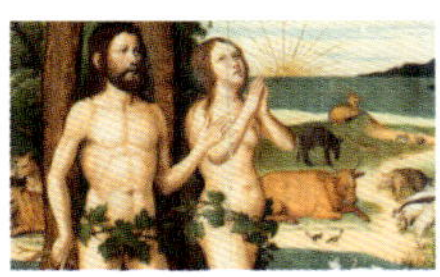

14. The *Creation* panel
p. 36

BAROQUE

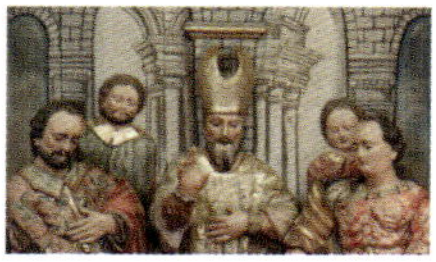

15. ***Marriage of the Virgin Mary***
p. 38

19th and 20th CENTURIES

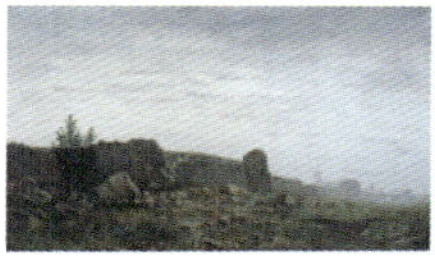

16. ***The Ramparts Around Girona***
p. 40

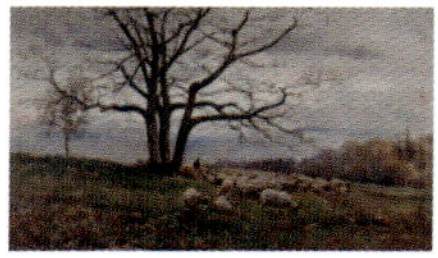

17. ***Flock of Sheep in a Field***
p. 42

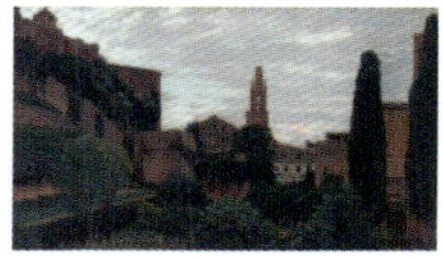

18. ***Girona***
p. 44

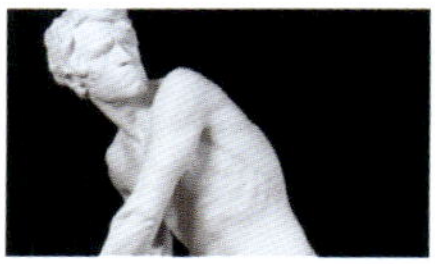

19. ***Against the Invader***
p. 46

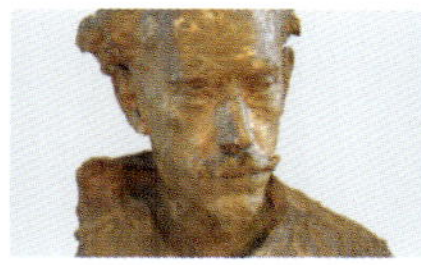

20. ***Bust of Prudenci Bertrana***
p. 48

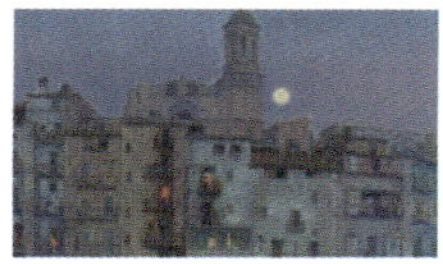

21. ***Full Moon at Girona***
p. 50

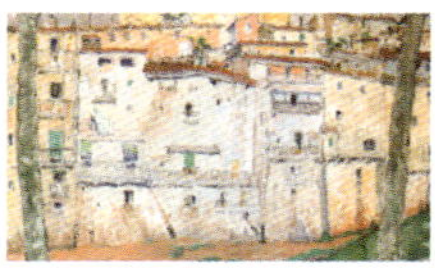

22. ***The Onyar River in Girona [By the River Bank]***
p. 52

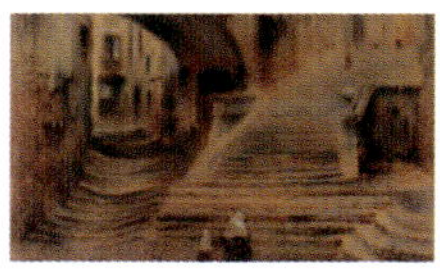

23. ***Stairway to Sant Martí***
p. 54

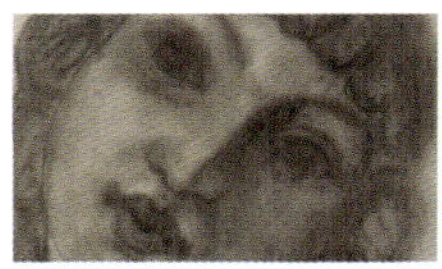

24. ***Head of a Woman***
p. 56

GIRONA ART MUSEUM FLOOR PLAN
p. 60

1. THE FIRST CHRISTIAN STONE

This irregularly shaped stone, chipped on all its sides, is a fragment of a gravestone found in the ruins of Empúries (Baix Empordà). Empúries, the outstanding spot on the Catalan coast where the Greeks and Romans successively landed, is possibly also the place where the early Christians set foot on Girona soil. The records of his martyrdom show that Saint Felix of Girona preached here shortly before being sacrificed in the city. The **gravestone** is an austere sample of the art of the early centuries of Christianity, which emerged under the persecution. It bears the Latin inscription "in Xto. Maxime ave vale". *Ave vale* is the Roman greeting, and Maximus is the name of the deceased, but its uniqueness lies in the fact that he died *in Xto*. For the first time, the name of Christ appears in Empúries, accompanied by alpha and omega, the beginning and the end of all things.

FRAGMENT OF AN EARLY CHRISTIAN GRAVESTONE

Fourth century
Carvings in marble
36 x 31 x 7 cm
Empúries. L'Escala (Alt Empordà)
Diocese of Girona Collection. Reg. no. MDG 859

FLOOR 1
Room 1

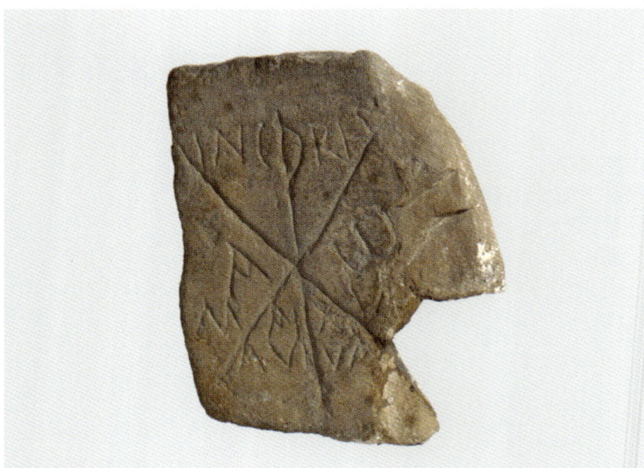

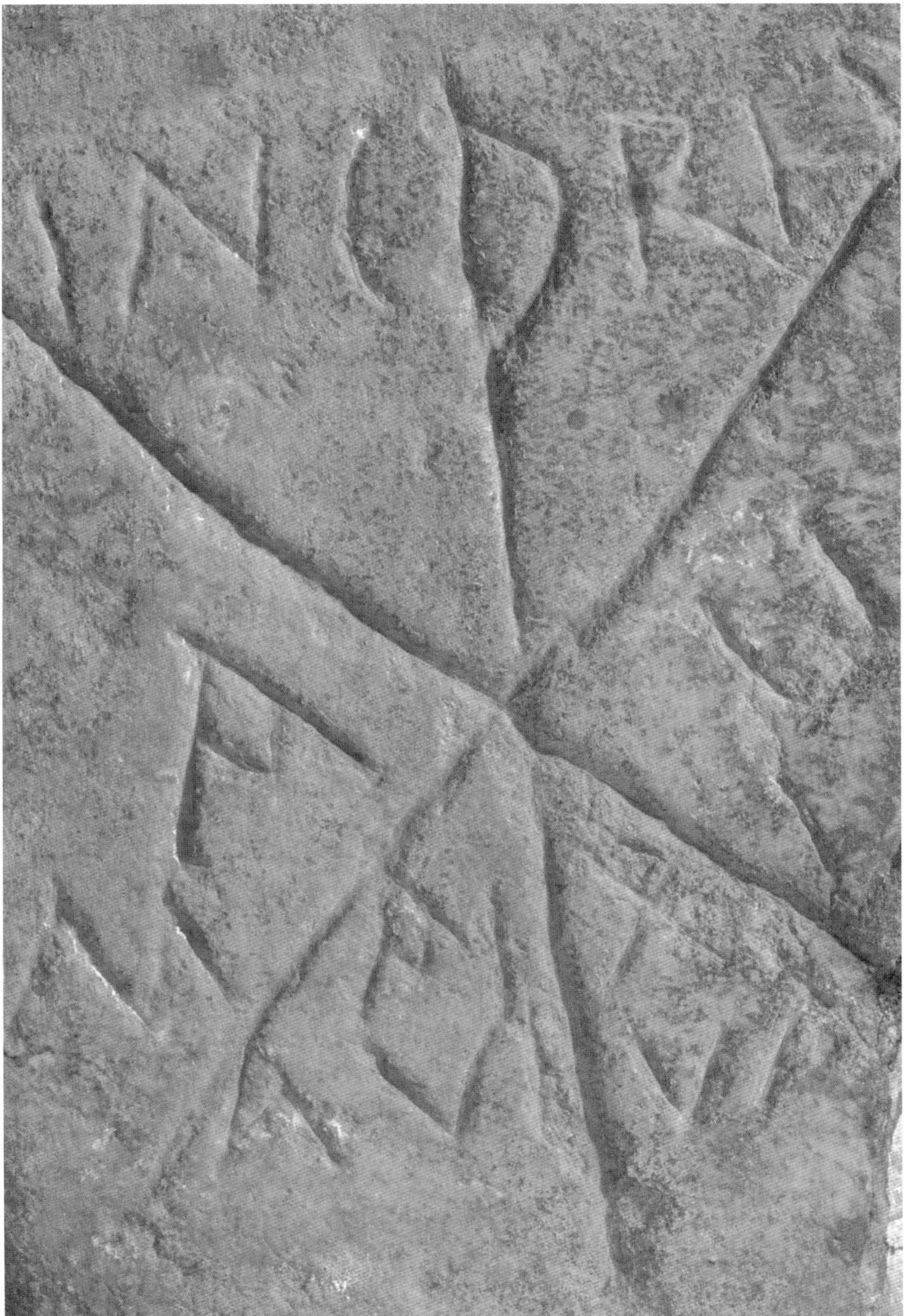

2. TRAVELLING ALTAR

According to legend, the imposing Benedictine monastery of Sant Pere de Rodes (Alt Empordà) is said to have held, in the early seventh century, the remains of Saint Peter, moved from Rome by order of the Pope, and was visited by Charlemagne in the year 778. These events are featured in Verdaguer's poem *Canigó*. Among the objects of the monastic site saved from being sacked is this portable **altar stone**, on which the abbots and monks said mass during their travels. The wood of this rectangular piece is covered with thin sheets of embossed silver. Inscriptions and ornamental elements accumulate until filling all the spaces. In the middle there is another rectangle of black and burnished slate, which is the actual altar stone, the essential altar under which the relics of the martyrs, indispensable for the liturgy of the Eucharistic sacrifice, were hidden.

PORTABLE ALTAR OF SANT PERE DE RODES

Tenth century
Wood, slate and embossed silver
22 x 14 x 2.5 cm
Monastery of Sant Pere de Rodes. El Port de la Selva (Alt Empordà)
Diocese of Girona Collection. Reg. no. MDG 20

FLOOR 1
Room 1

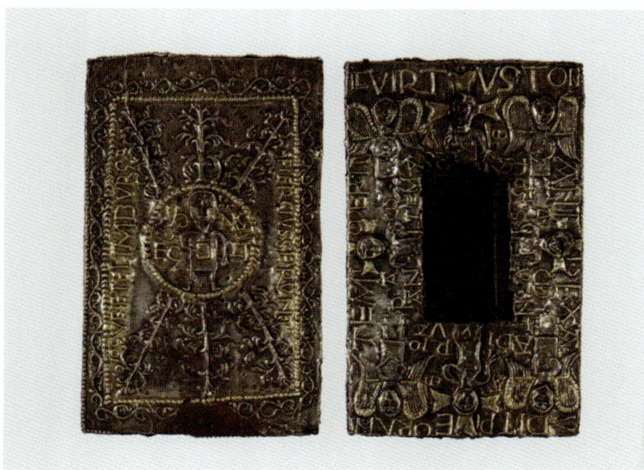

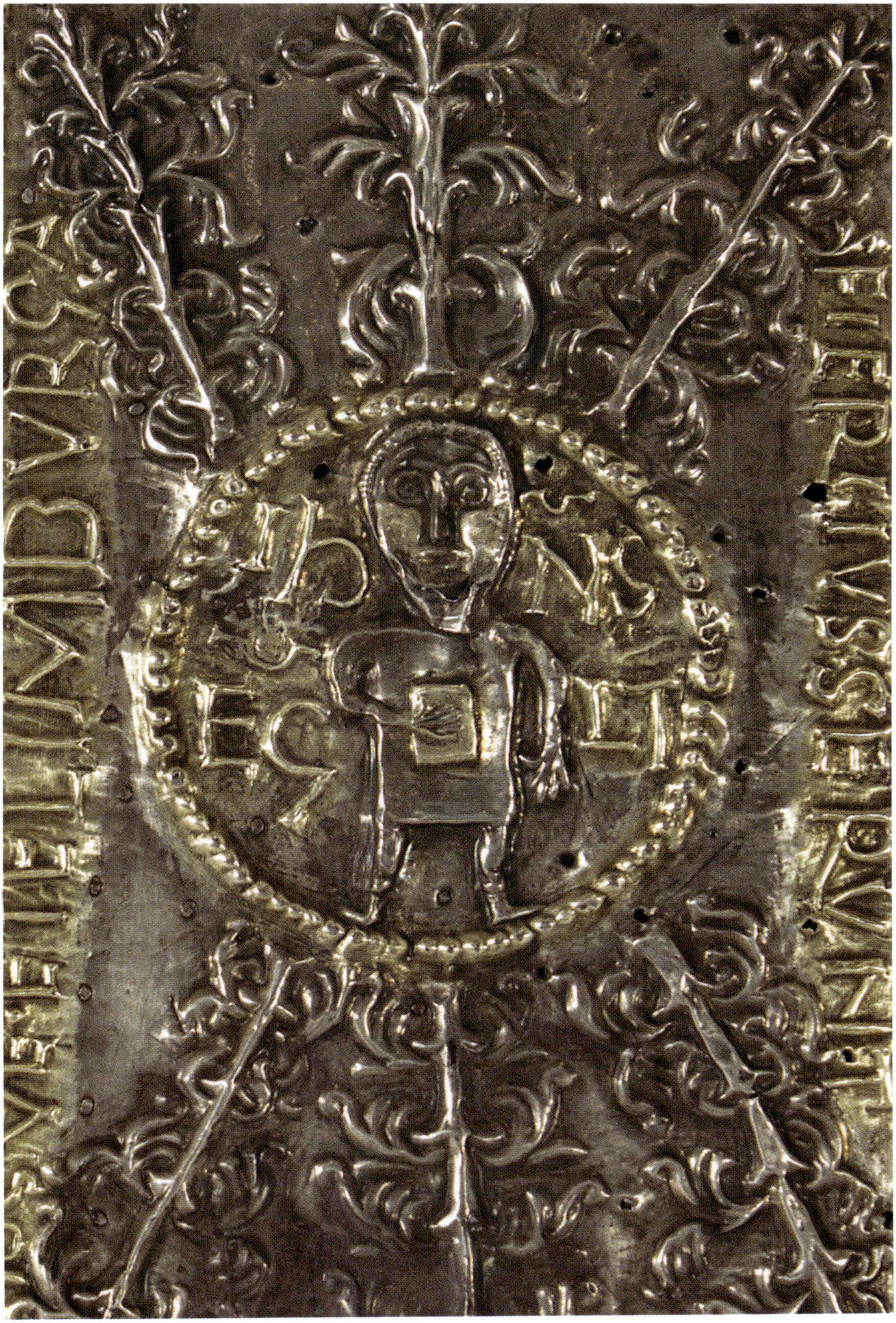

3. THE MONKS' PROCESSION

The Benedictine monks lived in the monastery of Sant Miquel de Cruïlles (Baix Empordà) for nine hundred years, from the early twelfth century to the confiscation of ecclesiastical property. This tempera-painted wooden **beam** must have been the main piece of a primitive baldachin placed on the high altar of the Romanesque church. At the front there is a procession or liturgical ceremony, with monks who might be from the same monastery or those who, presided over by the Bishop of Siponto, went in 663 to Monte Gargano, where the worship of the archangel Saint Michael began. The figures of the clergymen move slowly, with their heads held high and their mouths slightly open, in a singing gesture. The Gregorian chants that medieval monks introduced have survived identical until today and still seem to emerge from the depths of this beam with the vibrations of its centuries-old harmony.

CRUÏLLES BEAM

FLOOR 1
Room 3

c. 1200
Tempera on wood. 14 x 371 x 9 cm
Monastery of Sant Miquel de Cruïlles.
Cruïlles, Monells i Sant Sadurní de l'Heura
(Baix Empordà)
Diocese of Girona Collection. Reg. no. MDG 2

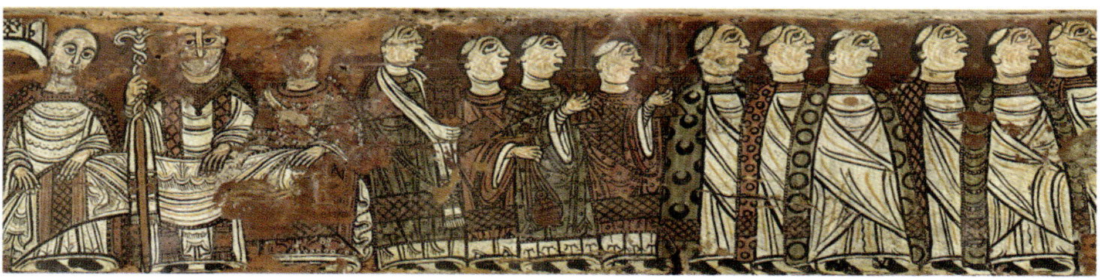

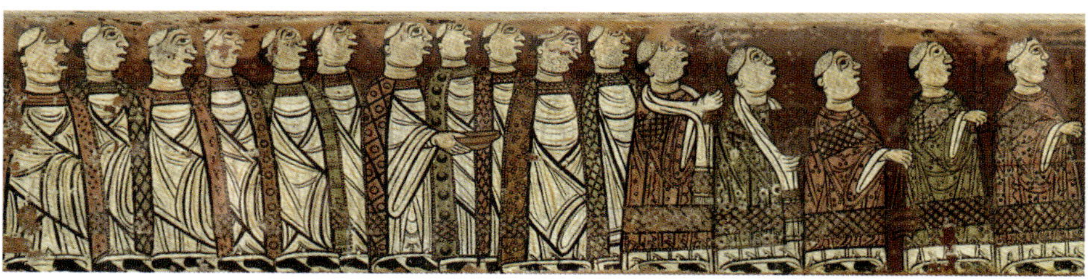

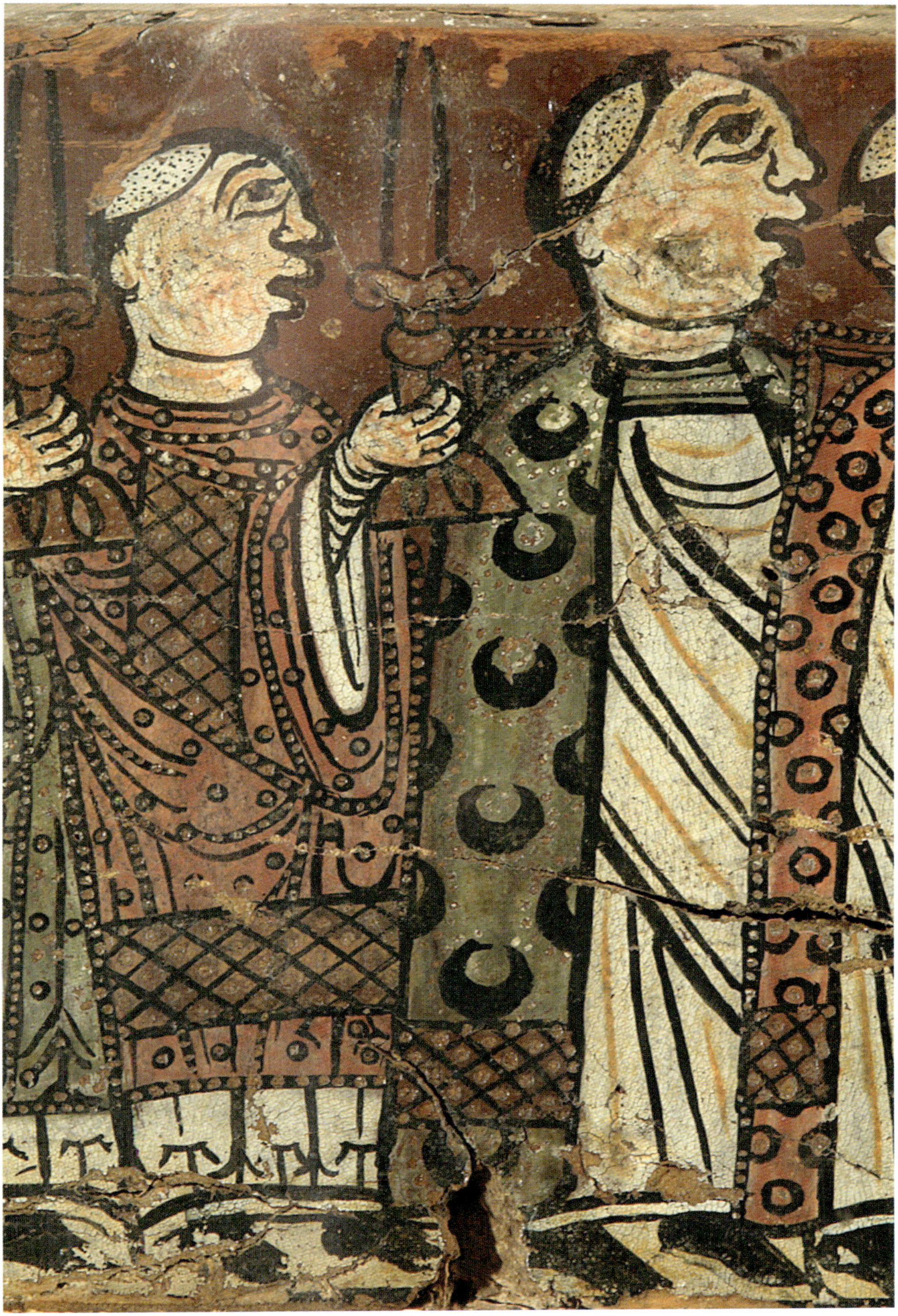

4. THE BLACK AND WHITE GOSPEL

This large codex, from the former collegiate church of Sant Feliu in Girona, is a characteristic example of the books produced in medieval scriptoria. In Ripoll (Ripollès) two bibles were made that are among the masterpieces of European miniature of their time: that of Ripoll, today in the Vatican Library in Rome, and that of Sant Pere de Rodes, today in the National Library of Paris. This more modest **book of homilies** can be related to the two famous bibles and contains the text of a homily by the Venerable Bede, an English monk of the seventh and eighth centuries, unknown until it was found written here. However, the main attraction of the volume lies in its illustrations, related to passages from the gospels; they are drawings completely devoid of colour and where all the expressive strength comes from the rigour of the line, drawn schematically with black ink on the broken white of the parchment.

BEDE'S BOOK OF HOMILIES

Eleventh century
Ink on parchment
35.5 x 28 x 10 cm
Church of Sant Feliu. Girona (Gironès)
Diocese of Girona Collection. Reg. no. MDG 44

FLOOR 1
Room 3

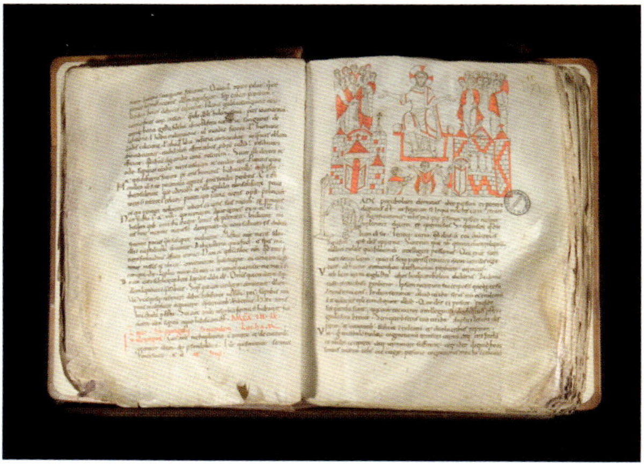

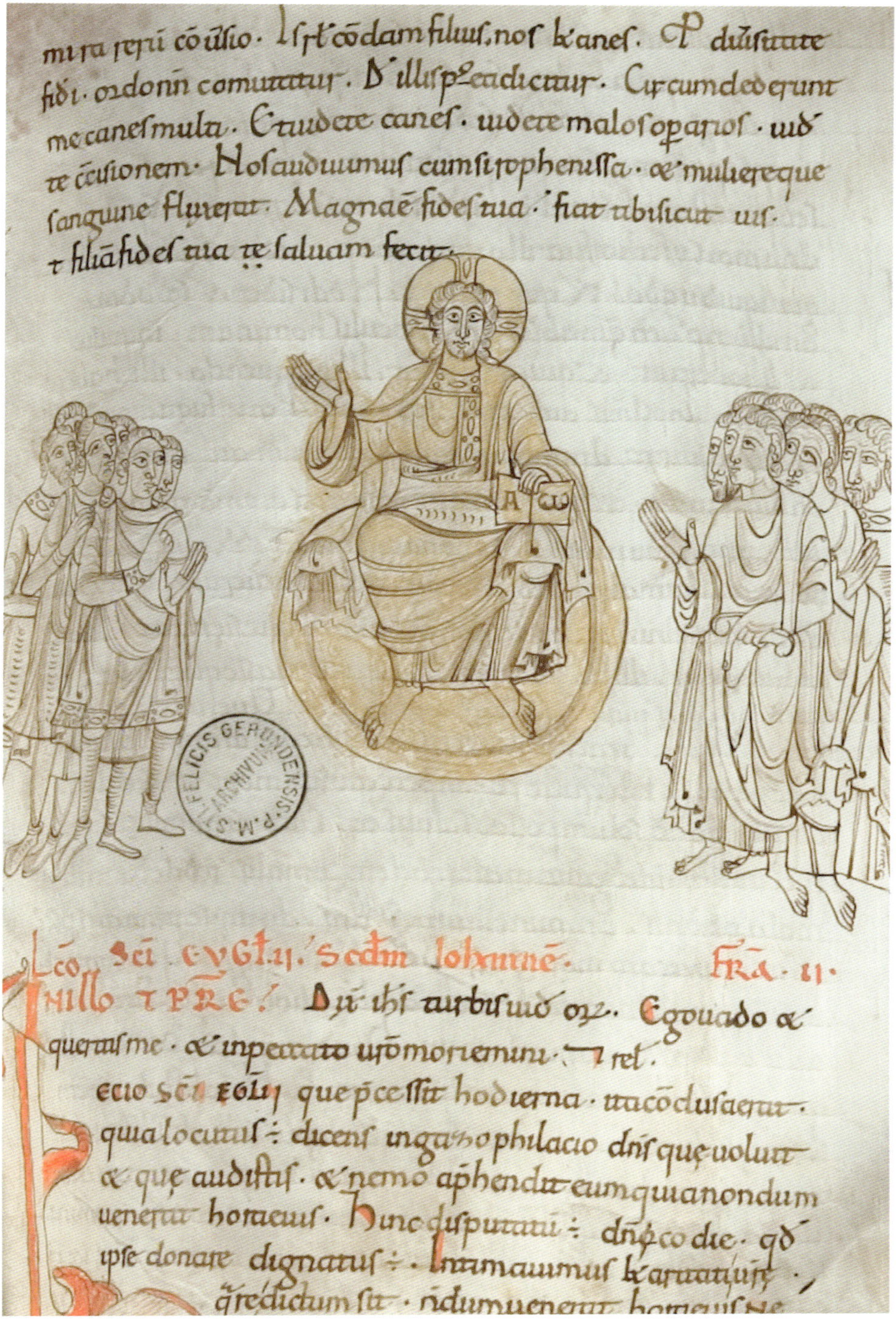
mira sepi coilio. Isti quidam filius, nos kanes. Et diuisitate
fidi. ordonn comutatur. De illis per ea dicitur. Circumdederunt
me canes multi. Et uidete canes. uidete malos operarios. uide
te concisionem. Hos audiuimus cum sirophenissa. et muliere que
sanguine fluxerat. Magna est fides tua. fiat tibi sicut uis.
filia fides tua te saluam fecit.

LECTIO SCI EVGLII SECUNDUM IOHANNEM. FRA. II.
IN ILLO TEMPORE. Dixit ihs turbis iudeorum. Ego uado et
queritis me. et in peccato uestro moriemini. Et rel.
LECTIO SCI EVGLII que precessit hodierna. ita conclusa est.
quia locutus est dicens in gazophilacio dns que uoluit
et que audistis. et nemo aprehendit eum quia nondum
uenerat hora eius. Hinc disputatum est. dno pro co die. quod
ipse donare dignatus est. Intimauimus karitati uestrae.
quare dictum sit. nondum uenerat hora eius. Ne

5. A NATIVITY SCENE ON THE WALL

This **mural painting** has been arranged here as it was extracted from the original site: the apse of the Romanesque church of Pedrinyà (Baix Empordà). It is anonymous, and it is difficult to attribute and date it. The vault is presided over by the *Maiestas Domini*, the image of Christ seated on a throne, as described in the Book of Revelation, surrounded by the symbolic animals of the four evangelists. Below, in a semicircle, are the successive scenes of the Mystery of the Incarnation: the Annunciation to Mary, the Visitation of Mary to Elizabeth, the Nativity, and the Annunciation to the Shepherds; everything suggests that the missing fragment corresponded to the Adoration of the Wise Men. However, these biblical scenes are not separated from each other, but are all shown together, as in the simultaneous setting of a popular nativity scene. Christ's ascent into heaven on the apse contrasts with the simplicity of the episodes related to his coming to Earth.

MASTER OF PEDRINYÀ
(late twelfth century)
Apse of Pedrinyà

Late twelfth century -
early thirteenth century
Fresco transferred to canvas
460 x 335 x 227 cm
Church of Sant Andreu
de Pedrinyà. La Pera (Baix
Empordà)
Diocese of Girona Collection. Reg. no. MDG 1

FLOOR 1
Room 4

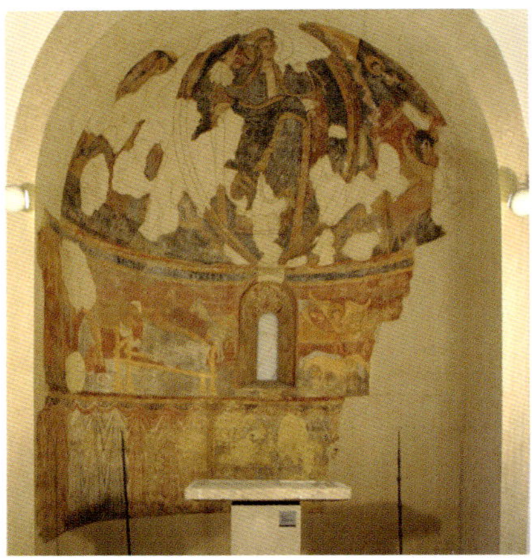

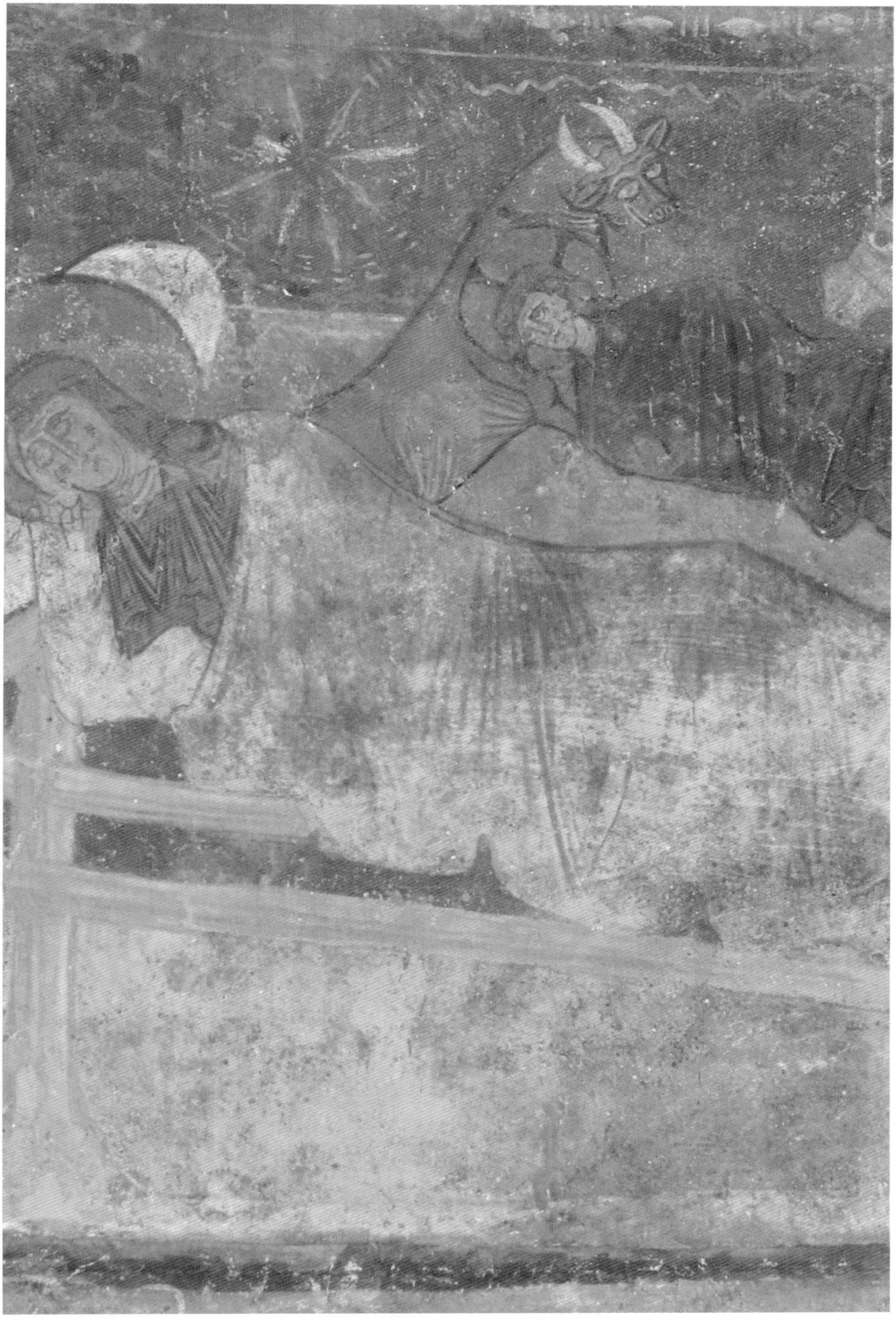

6. THE SYMBOL OF A COMMITMENT

This stone column comes from Carrer de Calderers in Girona. The animal climbing up it is a lion, but popular legend identifies it as a **lioness**. The shaft supported the roof beam of a hostel, located by the road, and to touch the animal's backside people had to stand on tiptoe. For many years, outsiders entering the city and stopping at the hostel were ironically warned of the prerequisite for being considered a citizen: "You cannot be a resident of Girona until you've kissed the lion's backside." This is how the gesture of kissing the stone beast became the symbol of integration and civic commitment. A replica of this piece, set on the street in its former location, is offered as a representative icon to which tourists and visitors are invited to pay their ancestral tribute to ensure their return to the city in the future.

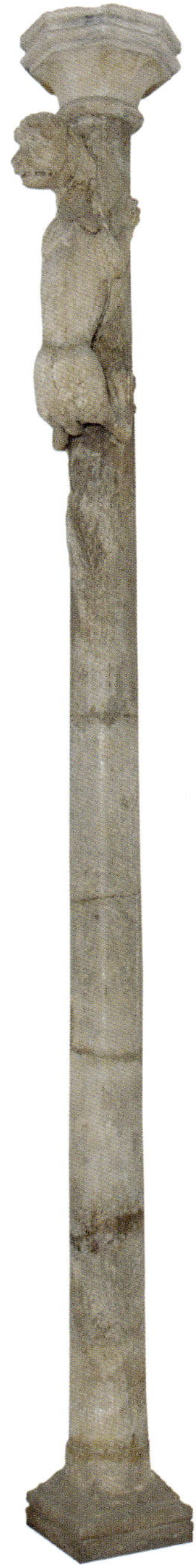

THE LIONESS

Second half of the thirteenth century - late fourteenth century
Girona limestone
372 x 46 x 38 cm
Carrer de Calderers, 1. Girona (Gironès)
Girona Provincial Council Art Collection. Reg. no. 1.756

FLOOR 1
Room 4

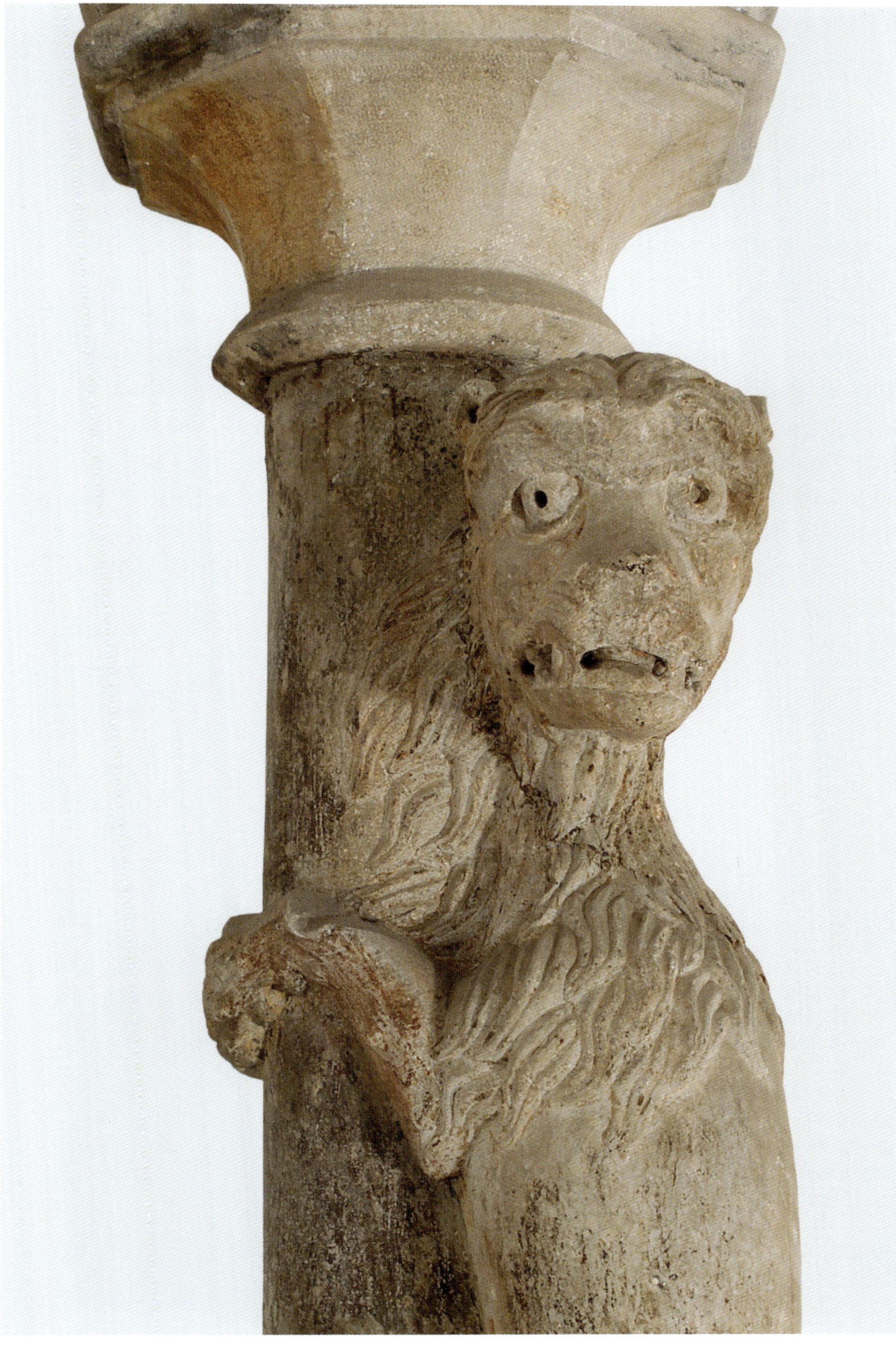

7. THE LONG WAIT OF THE CENTURIES

This enigmatic statue of the Virgin comes from the convent of Sant Francesc in Girona, which was situated on the left bank of the Onyar River, the current location of Carrer Nou. Some say that for a long time it was in an outdoor niche, over the gateway in the wall leading to the upper part of the Rambla, at one of the entrances to the city. Sitting in silent wait, with her hands on her knees, this **Virgin** portrayed before childbirth has an expressionless face, as if concentrated on the mystery within her. The statue parallels that of Notre-Dame de Bon-Espoir in Dijon and many other nursing Madonnas that some connect with the Celtic Earth goddess, worshipped on sacred sites by the druids and finally Christianised and turned into the virgin who will give birth to a divine and human child at the same time, saviour of the world and humanity. Thus the hopes of the patriarchs and prophets who for centuries had dreamed of the coming of the Desire of all Nations culminate in this impassive figure.

OUR LADY OF HOPE

First quarter of the fifteenth century
Polychrome alabaster
80 x 31 x 31 cm
Convent of Sant Francesc d'Assís. Girona (Gironès)
Girona Provincial Council Art Collection. Reg. no. 1.830

FLOOR 1
Room 5

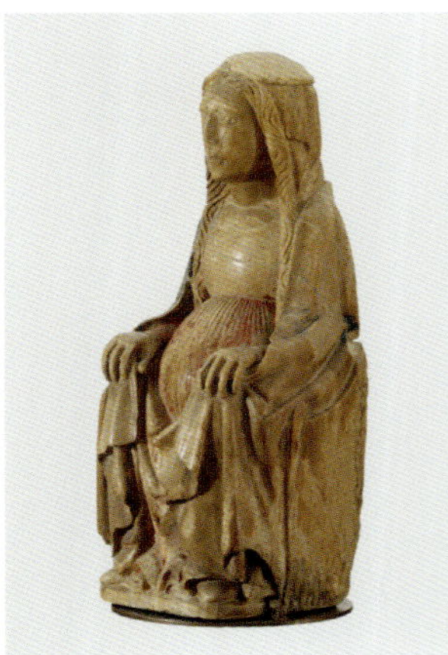

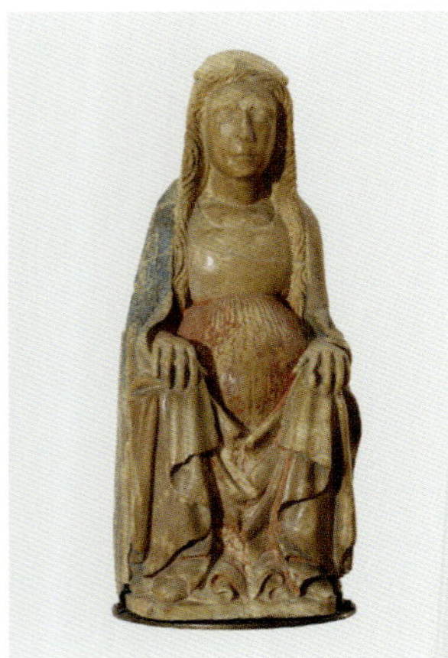

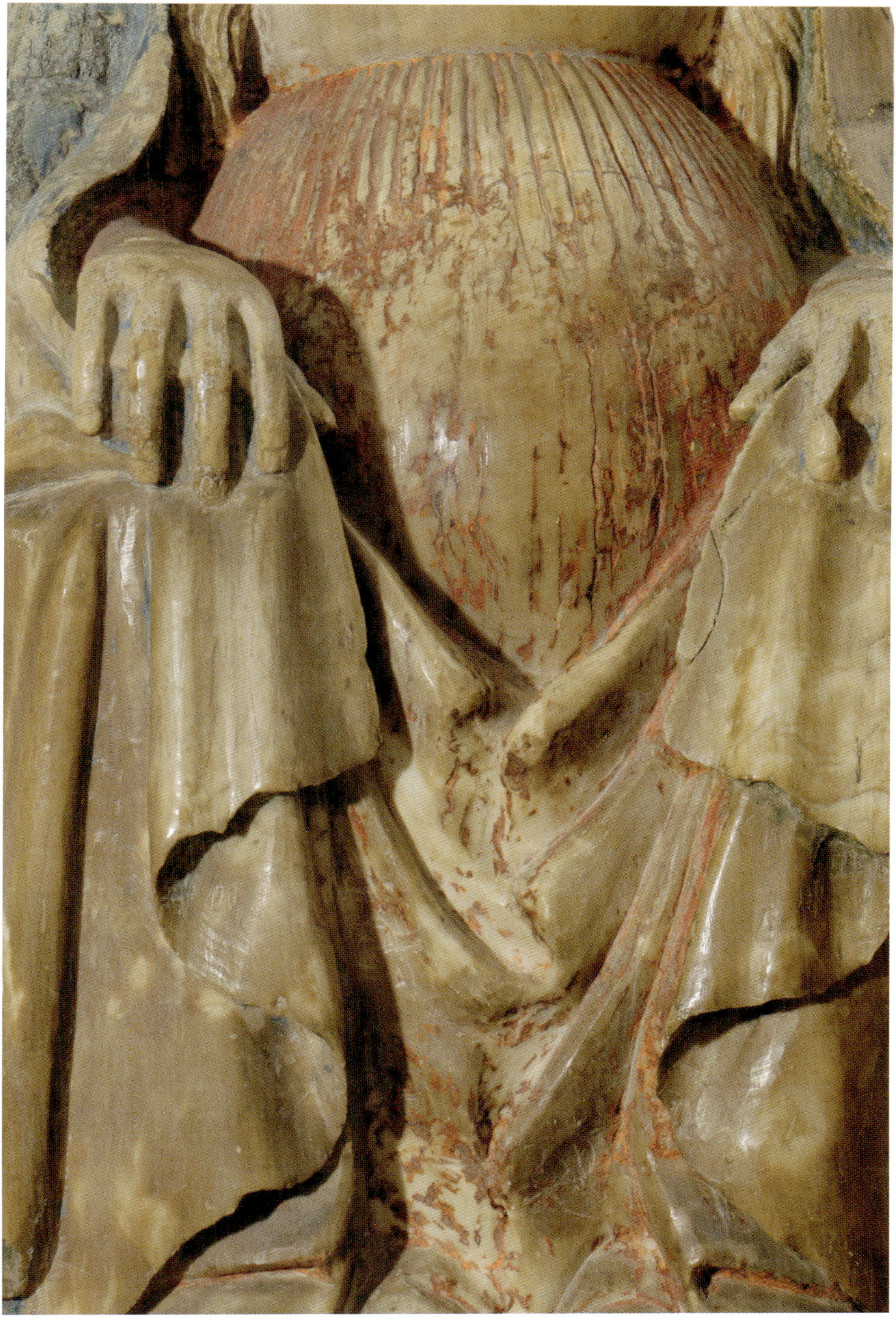

8. THE TRANSFIGURATION OF PAIN

These five limestone pieces —Jesus, the Virgin, Saint John and the two thieves— crowned the lintel of the door that connected the cloister of Girona Cathedral with the clergymen's cemetery. The sculptures reflect a historical transition: Romanesque in the treatment of the naked bodies, the folds of the garments are a step towards the enhanced realism of the Gothic style. They are, therefore, the result of a time of change, and are due both to the canons of the style that was coming to an end and to the innovations of the one that was beginning to take root. However, the realism of the ensemble does not go beyond the folds of the garments: this **Calvary** of hieratic figures seems to be set in the purest unreality. Jesus has a geometrically stylised beard, braided hair in the shape of a royal crown, and is resting on a trunk with symmetrical pruned branches. The human pain etched upon his face seems to be transfigured into placid and serene majesty.

MASTER BARTOMEU (second half of the thirteenth century)
Calvary

Late thirteenth century
Polychrome limestone
111 x 101 x 34 cm
Cathedral of Santa Maria. Girona (Gironès)
Girona Provincial Council Art Collection. Reg. no.1.725-1.729

FLOOR 1
Room 5

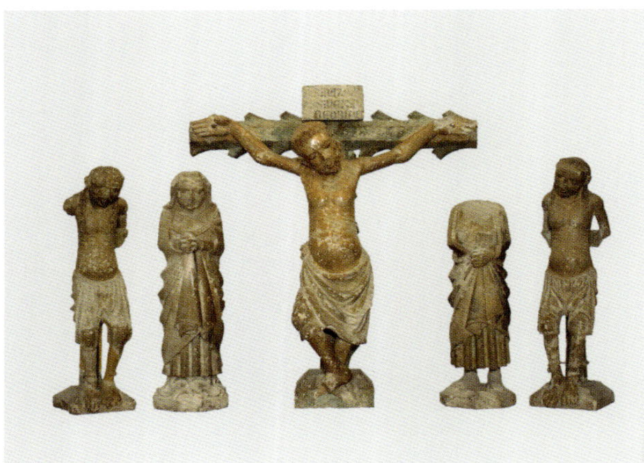

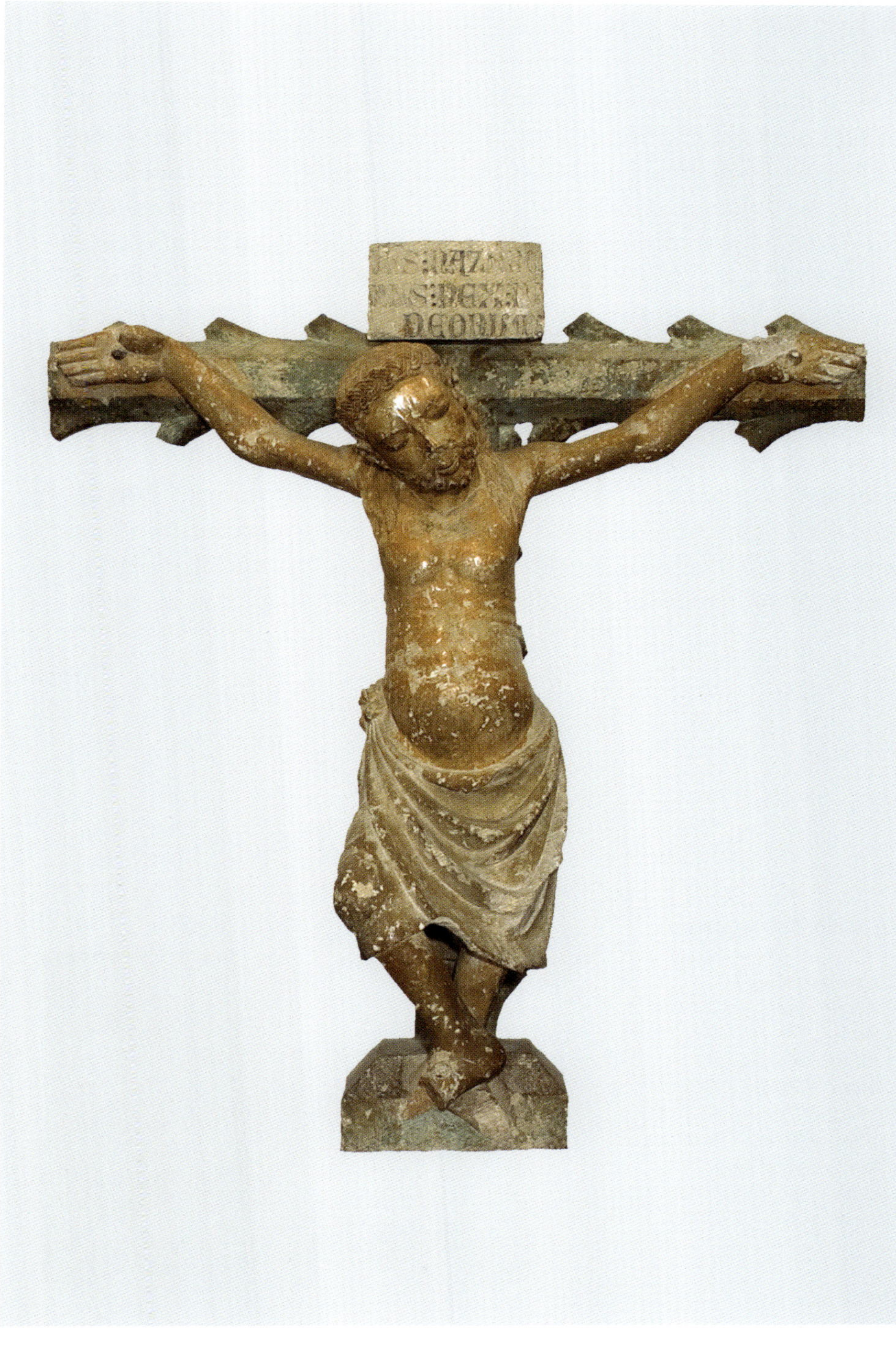

9. THE MARTYRS' CALENDAR

This vellum codex was made by the miniaturists of Prague who worked at the court of King Wenceslaus IV of Bohemia. Its owner, the Viceroy of Naples, bequeathed it to the Cistercian monastery of Poblet and, when the library was disbanded due to the confiscation of ecclesiastical property, two monks deposited it in the convent of the Bernardine Sisters in Girona. During the Spanish Civil War it was exhibited at the Jeu de Paume in Paris. It features an account of sacrifice of the martyrs, that is, a **martyrology**, arranged in the form of a calendar to be sung every day in the choirs of cathedrals or read in the refectories of monasteries. Conceived in a moment of splendour for Central European arts, alongside the text, it boasts seven hundred and fifty miniatures in red and black Gothic lettering. The lush vegetation of the borders links the medallions, where the raw scenes of martyrdom are depicted in very vivid colours on a gold background that places the historical or legendary characters in a sphere of magic and mystery.

Usuard's Martyrology

Fifteenth century
Polychrome and miniated vellum
46.9 x 33.8 x 5.2 cm
Library of Pedro Antonio de Aragón, monastery of Poblet. Vimbodí i Poblet (Conca de Barberà)
Diocese of Girona Collection. Reg. no. MDG 273

FLOOR 1
Room 5

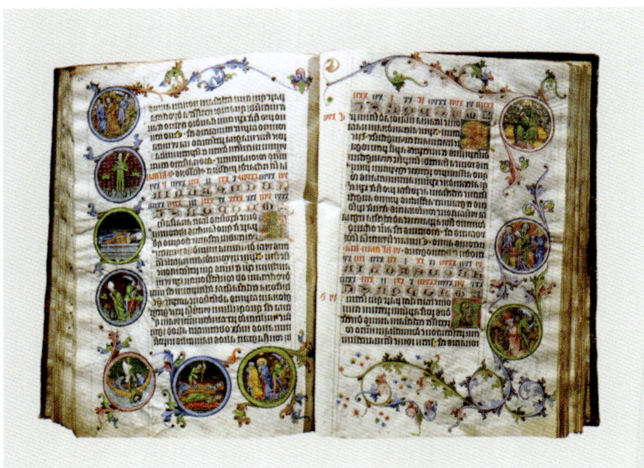

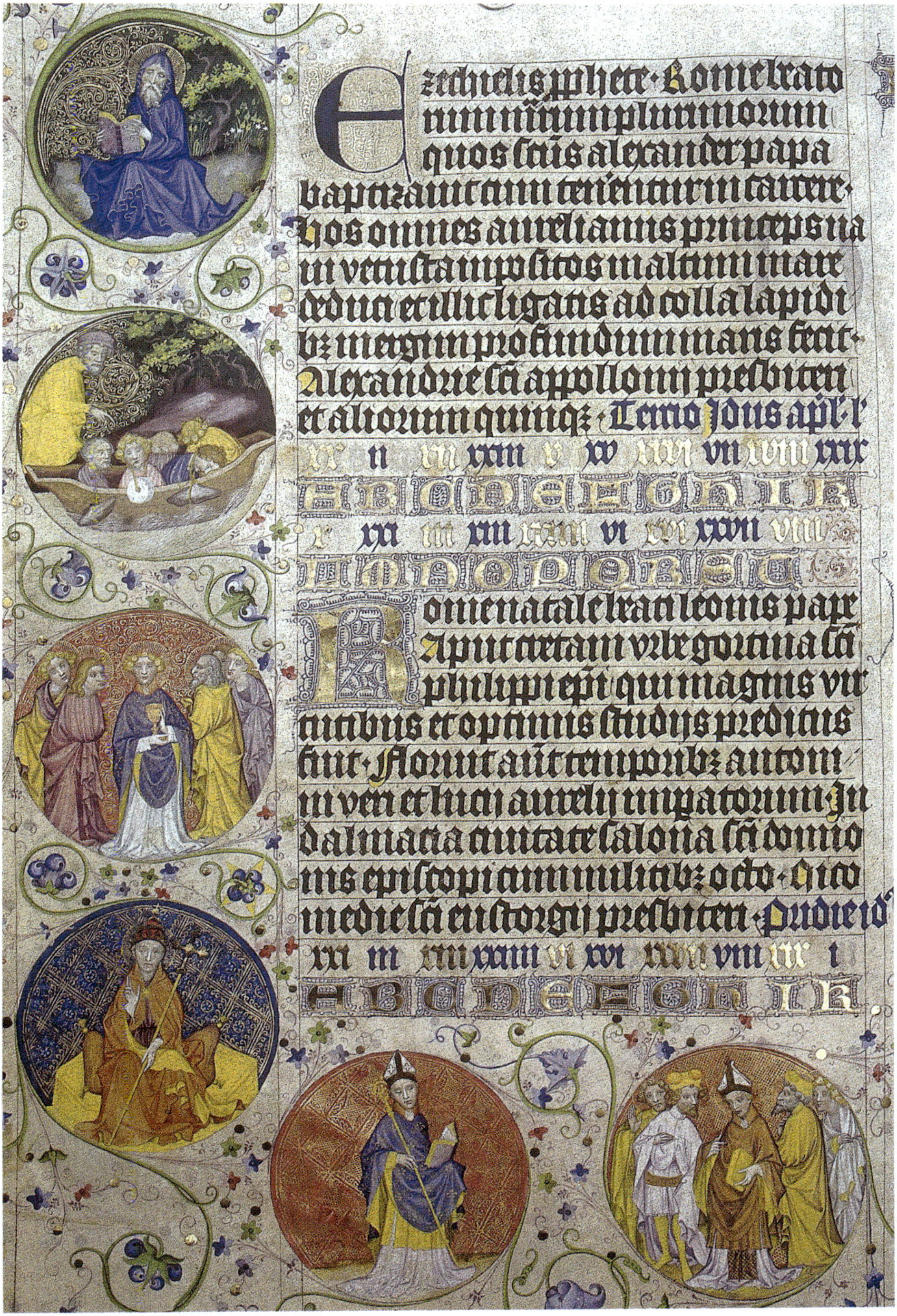

10. THE BATTLES OF THE ARCHANGEL

This **altarpiece** dedicated to Saint Michael, who presided over the Romanesque church of the monastery of Cruïlles (Baix Empordà), is the work of Lluís Borrassà, a citizen of Girona with a studio in Barcelona, who was the most important painter in Catalonia during his forty years of activity. Amidst natural landscapes and stylised architectures, the characters move in perfectly composed scenes. The colours form a real symphony of reds and oranges over the gold of the background and halo the scene with a spectral light, like dawn or sunset. Saint Michael is presented as the compassionate defender of souls, but also as a relentless conqueror of his enemies. Dressed in the armour of the medieval warrior who plunges his spear into the seven-headed dragon, the invincible archangel in combat leads the first great battle in history – that of Genesis – and also the last – that of Revelation –, as well as the perpetual struggle that the forces of good have waged against the intrigues of evil.

LLUÍS BORRASSÀ
(c. 1365 - c. 1425)
Altarpiece of Sant Miquel de Cruïlles

1416
Tempera on wood
556 x 330 cm
Monastery of Sant Miquel de Cruïlles. Cruïlles, Monells i Sant Sadurní de l'Heura (Baix Empordà)
Diocese of Girona Collection. Reg. no. MDG 291

FLOOR 1
Room 8

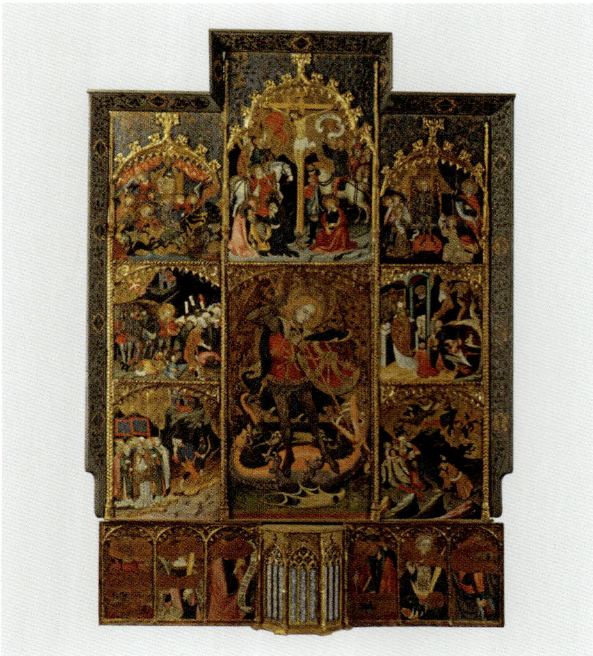

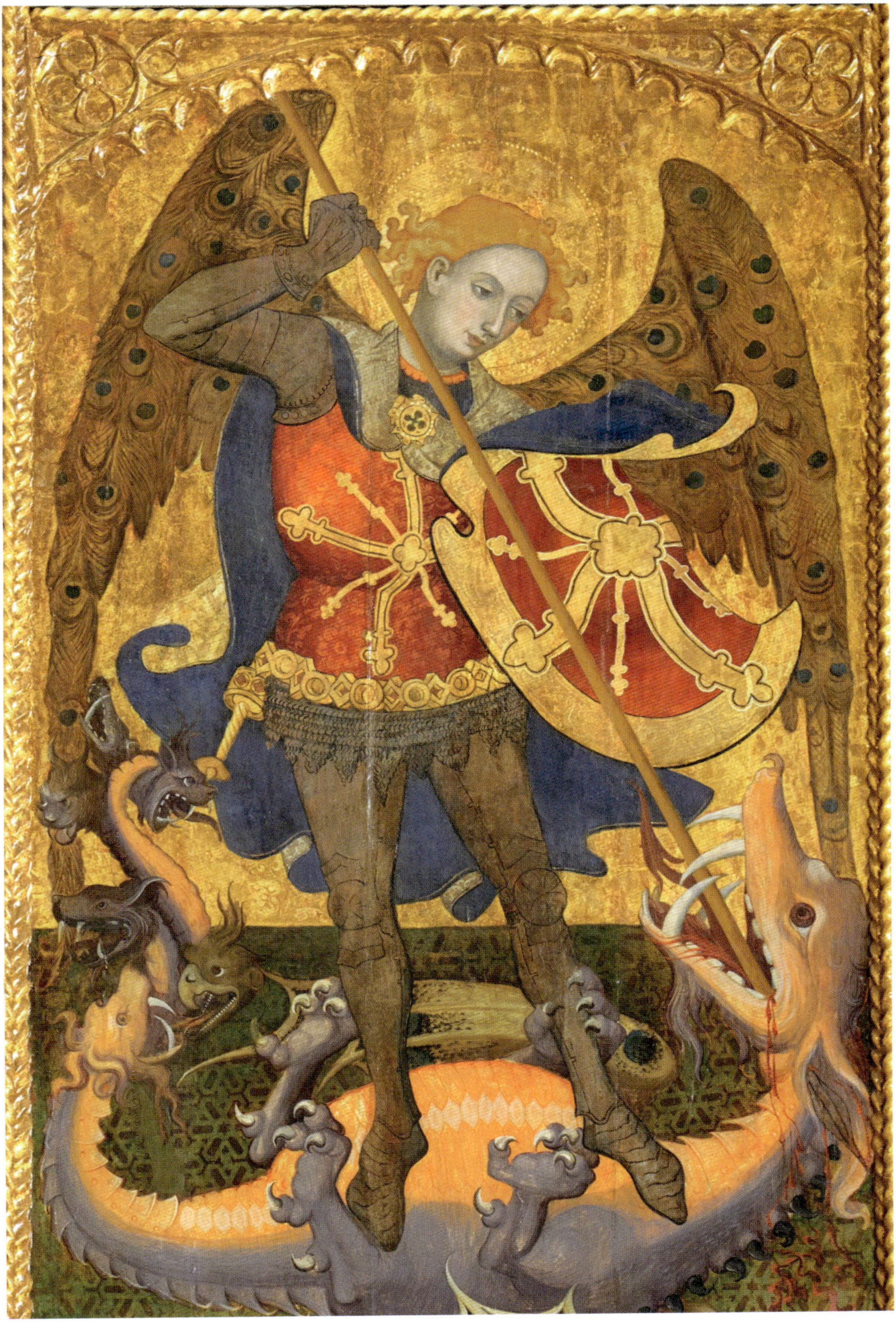

11. THE SAINTS DRESSED AS ORDINARY PEOPLE

This altarpiece presided for centuries over the altar of the small church of Púbol (Baix Empordà), which was, in fact, the castle chapel. Its owners, the Campllong Corberas, commissioned it to the painter Bernat Martorell, the best specialist of the time. He is responsible for the full integration of reality into art: he used the obligatory religious themes to portray the forms of civil life and introduced sacred or historical characters dressed like his contemporaries. In this **altarpiece** dedicated to Saint Peter, who presides over it with papal liturgical ornaments, you can admire the creative power in the treatment of the figure, the meticulous description of the surroundings and the clever use of light. On the reverse of the panels, sketches of black and white figures have been discovered, which, according to experts, are the oldest known charcoal drawings in the history of Catalan art.

BERNAT MARTORELL
(1390-1452)
Altarpiece of Sant Pere de Púbol

1437
Tempera on wood
490 x 370 cm
Church of Sant Pere de Púbol. La Pera (Baix Empordà)
Diocese of Girona Collection. Reg. no. MDG 289

FLOOR 1
Room 8

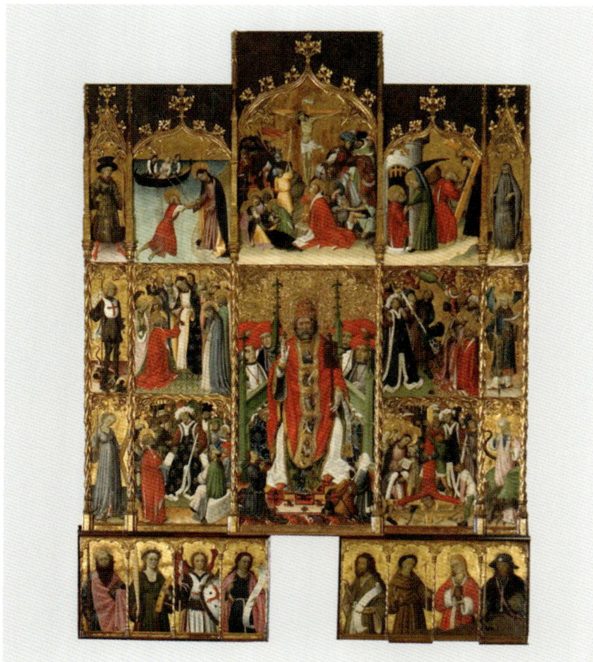

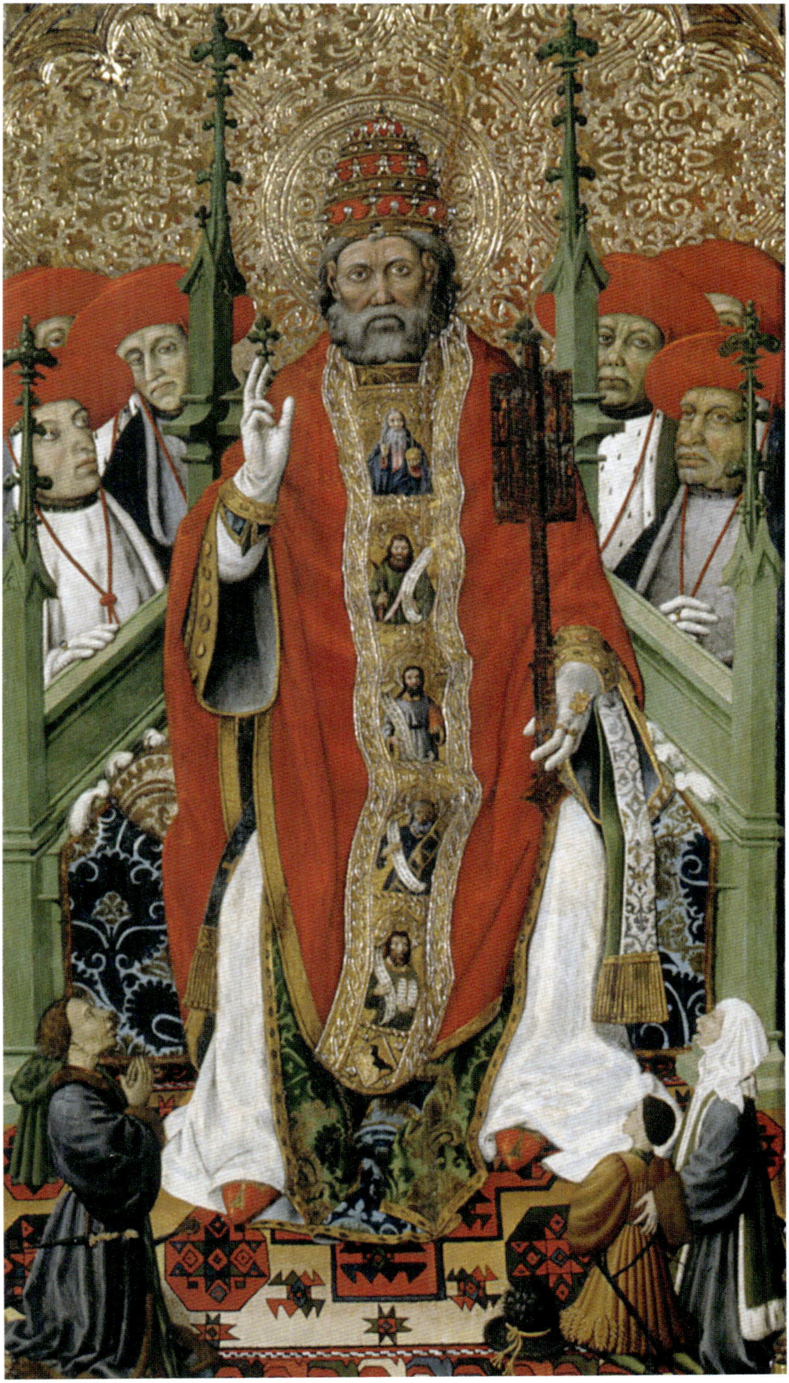

12. COMING FROM AFAR TO GO BEYOND

This **altarpiece**, now dismantled, occupied the apse of the Girona basilica of Sant Feliu until the Spanish Civil War in 1936. It took sixteen years to complete. The death of the German Perris de Fontaines, who had painted the bottom panel, led to the arrival in Girona of a new artist imbued with renovating fever: Joan de Burgunya, the son of a goldsmith from Strasbourg. He painted, in tempera and oil, the six panels that portray consecutive episodes of the preaching and martyrdom of Saint Felix of Girona, brutally sacrificed by the Romans in Girona and who became one of the most revered martyrs of the early Christian period. The veracity of the scenes painted by Burgunya coexists with the artificial and deliberate composition of the figures, the richness of the garments and the lavish scenery. The Strasbourg-born artist died too soon to be fully representative of the Renaissance, but everything shows that he was the first to set Catalan painting on a new path.

JOAN DE BURGUNYA (Borgonya) (1503 [doc.] - 1525)
***Preaching of Saint Felix in Girona*. Altarpiece of Sant Feliu**

1519-1520
Oil and tempera on wood
221 x 151 cm
Basilica of Sant Feliu. Girona (Gironès)
Diocese of Girona Collection. Reg. no. MDG 2.291

FLOOR 1
Room 9

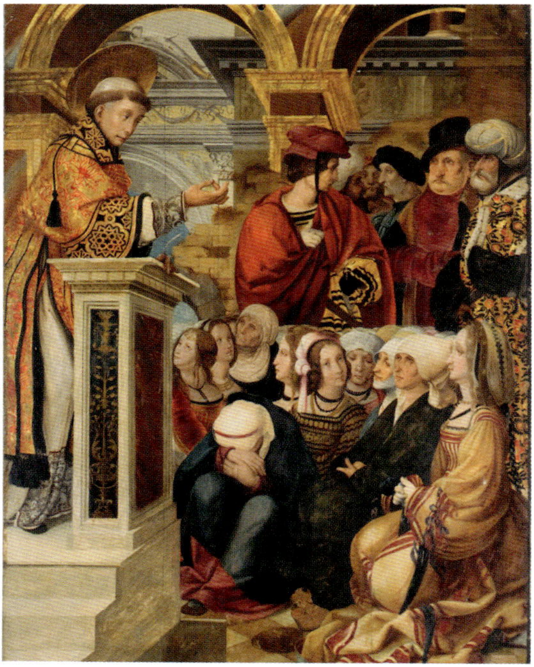

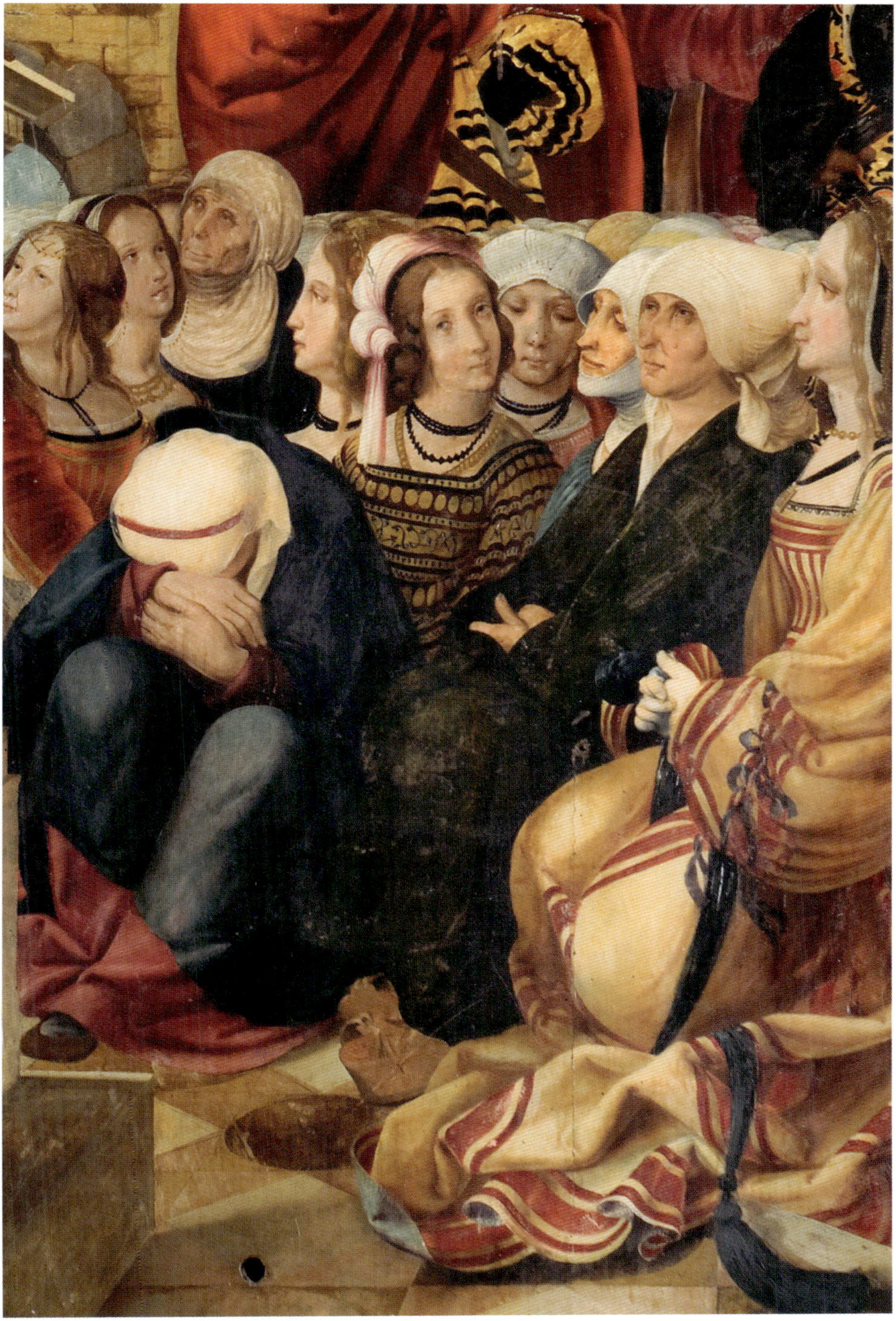

13. THE SECRET OF STAINED GLASS WINDOWS

These two wooden posts, unique in the world, are the first physical evidence of the work of medieval stained glass artists. On these previously whitewashed work tables punch and pigments were used to make the drawings as guides for the glass, cut to size and then assembled and set with lead. You can still see the holes of the nails that held the lead and the conventional signs used to mark the colours of each piece of glass. The value of the **work tables** is increased by the fact that Girona Cathedral houses the stained glass drawn and produced on them, which enables us to follow the production process and see the final result. The full splendour of the large Gothic stained glass windows was developed in silent patience on these pieces of wood, in which the opaque lines of the drawing belie the glory of the light that bursts in when the cathedral nave is flooded by the rays of the sun.

STAINED GLASSMAKER'S WORK TABLES

Fourteenth century
Tempera on wood
123 x 39 x 2.5 cm
Cathedral of Santa Maria.
Girona (Gironès)
Diocese of Girona Collection. Reg. no.MDG 279-280

FLOOR 2
L'Espai

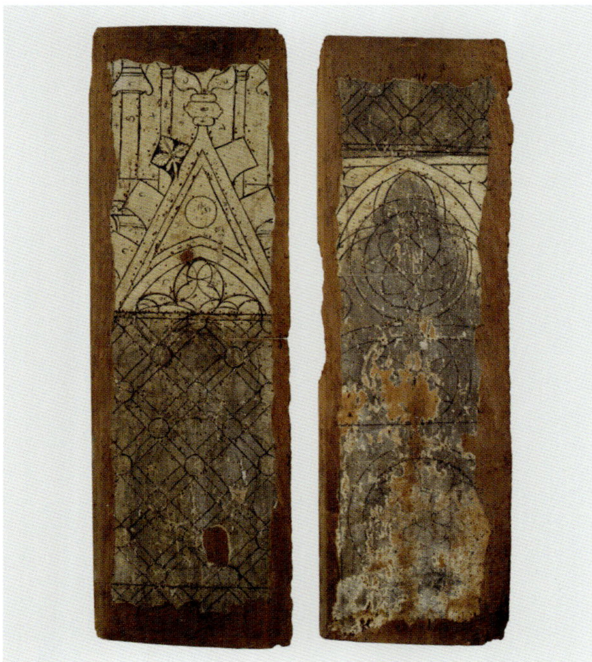

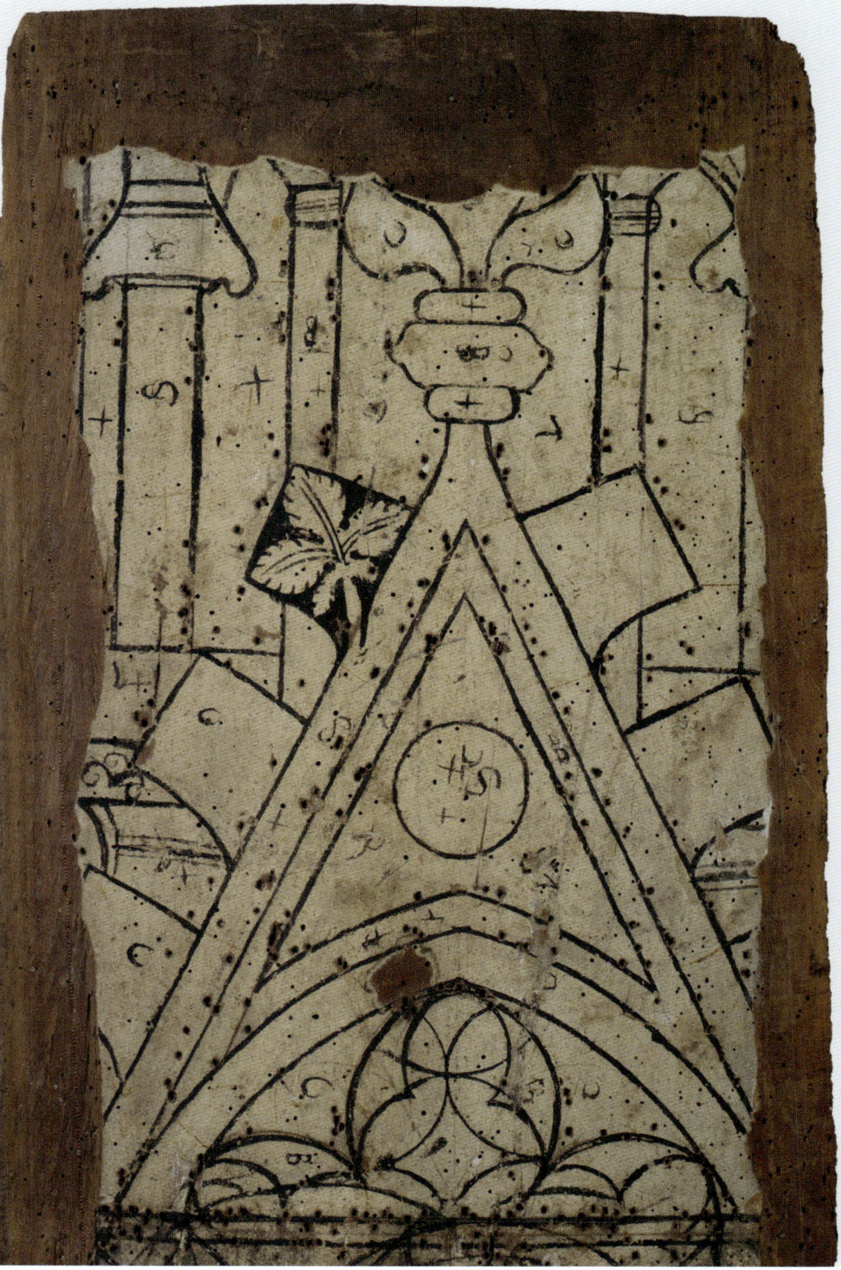

14. THE DUAL TENSION BETWEEN TWO WORLDS

This **altarpiece**, which presided over the parish church of Santa Maria de Segueró (Garrotxa), is one of many made in the region of Girona by the painter Pere Mates, with a studio established in the city; an artist who saw the arrival of the Renaissance and adhered to its postulates, but without completely breaking with tradition. These panels, the most mature of his work, portray episodes from the life of Mary, complemented by two parallel scenes about the beginning and end of the world. The Creation panel is of particular interest; the composition of the ensemble and the almost excessive realism of the details reflect a dual tension: the one that confronts humans with God after sin, underlined by the absolute passivity of vegetables and animals, and the one that the painter experiences between two equally contrasting styles. The last vestiges of Gothic style endeavour to strike a balance with the innovations of the Renaissance and join with the great currents of modernity.

Pere Mates
(c. 1490 - 1558)
THE *CREATION* PANEL.
Segueró altarpiece

c. 1530
Oil and tempera on wood
122 x 171 cm
Church of Santa Maria de Segueró. Beuda (Garrotxa)
Diocese of Girona Collection. Reg. no. MDG 380-383

FLOOR 2
Room 12

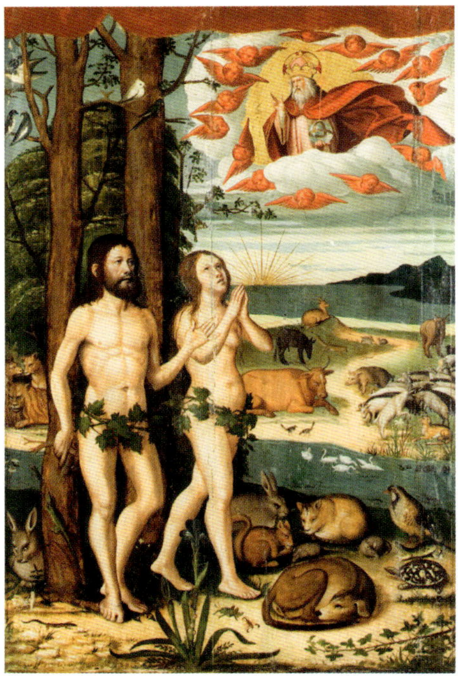

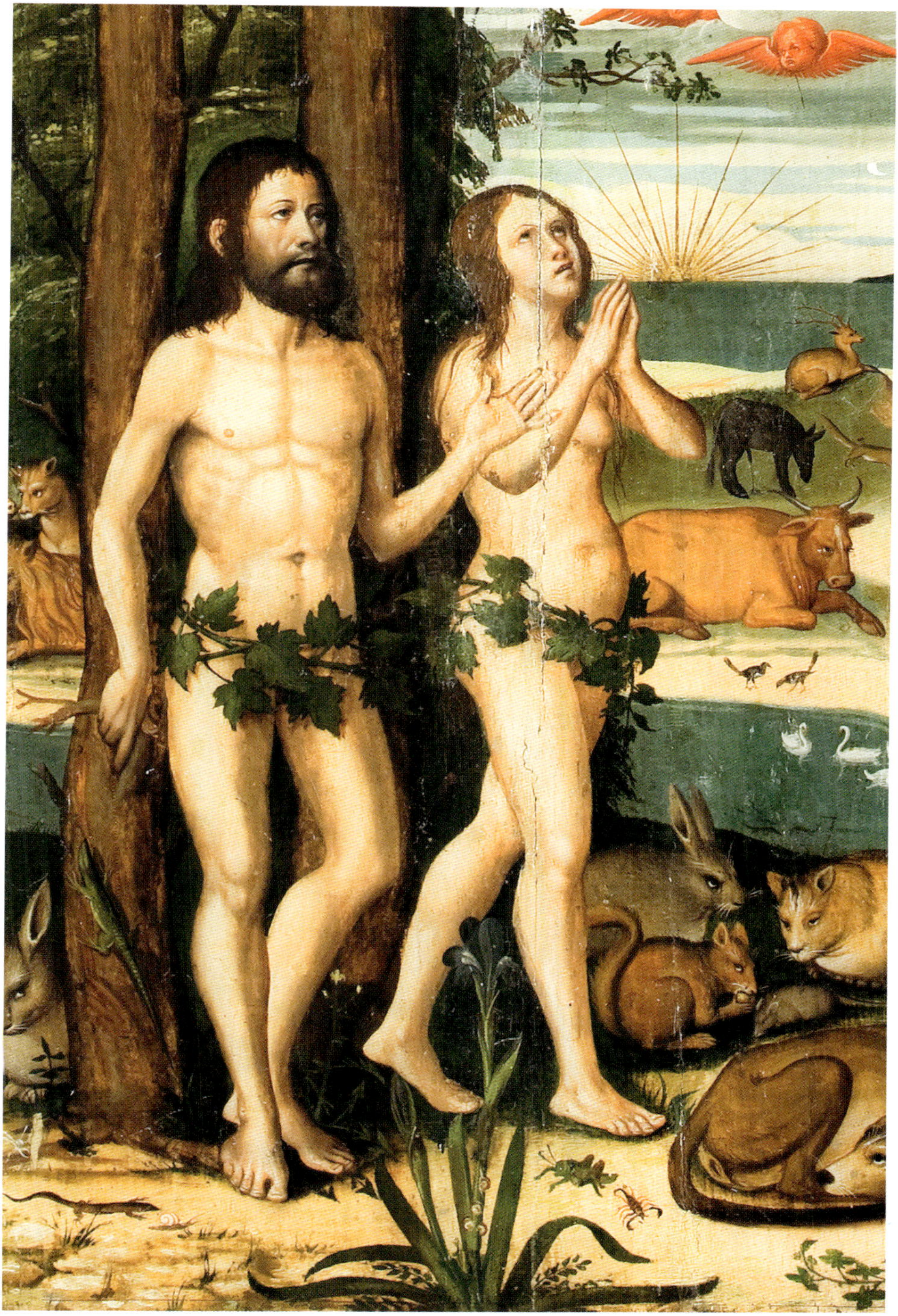

15. A WEDDING PORTRAIT

This sculptural group is only a fragment of the **altarpiece** of the Brotherhood of the Forsaken's altar in the basilica of Sant Feliu in Girona. It portrays the scene of the marriage of the Virgin according to the ritual of the Jewish people and is structured on two planes: in the foreground, Mary, Saint Joseph and the priest of the Law of Moses; further in, as if in an embossed setting, two witnesses to the ceremony, against the interior backdrop of the temple. As if they were dolls crammed into a toy box, the five figures fit into the niche to be present in the official image of the marriage. They are dressed in festive clothes, arranged in wide folds and decorative shapes and worked in bright colours on gold. Francesc Generes, a sculptor from Manresa temporarily established in Girona, created these volumes of polychrome wood in tempera and oil to immortalise the betrothal of Joseph and Mary with the expressive resources and sumptuous magnificence of Catalan baroque.

Francesc Generes [atrib.]
(1656 [doc.] - 1710)
MARRIAGE OF
THE VIRGIN MARY

1677
Gilded polychrome wood
220 x 134 x 44 cm
Basilica of Sant Feliu.
Girona (Gironès)
Diocese of Girona Collection. Reg. no. MDG 1.049-1.051

FLOOR 3
Room 14

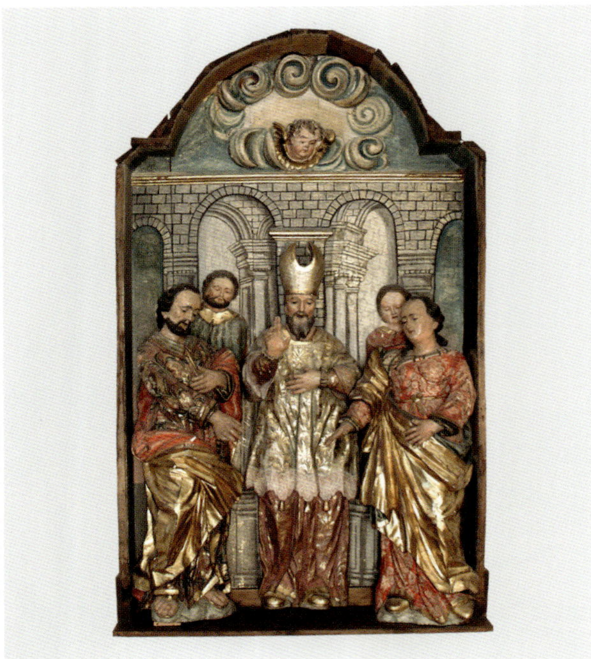

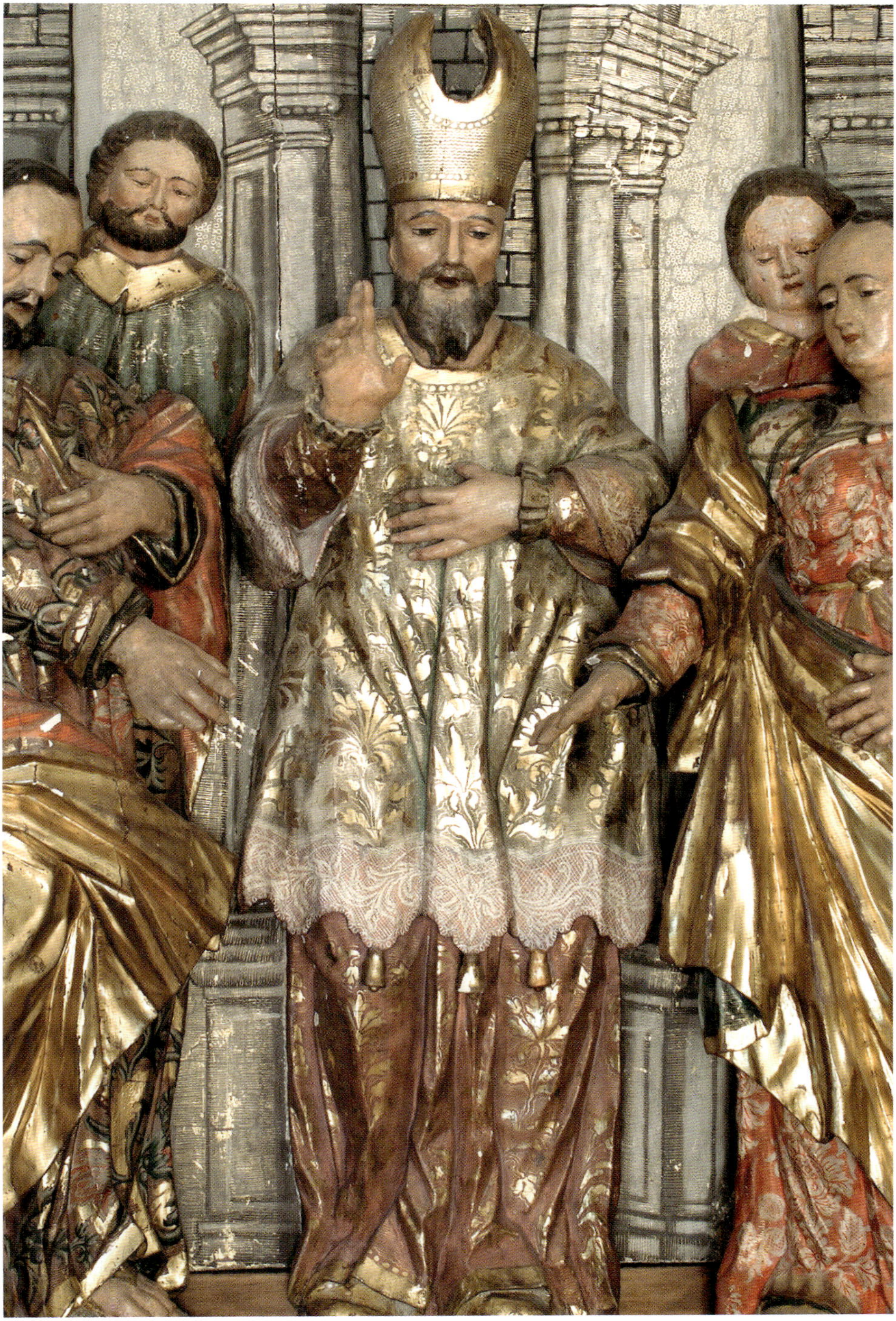

16. THE EAGLE, THE WALL AND THE BAY TREE

Born in Barcelona, Modest Urgell was a disciple of Ramon Martí i Alsina and, in Paris, of Gustave Courbet, but he eschewed the positivist realism of his teachers to enter a world of mystery and melancholy. Still attached to the canons of academicism, his work is, at the same time, a prelude to symbolism, and with it he achieved fame in Europe and America. This **allegorical painting** about the sieges of Girona by Napoleonic troops breaks all the moulds of epic representations – war scenes full of fire and blood –to show the desolate picture of the deserted walls and the silhouette of the city rising above a twilight sky. In the foreground, on the unsettled earth of the ditch, the sinister flight of a fleeing eagle evokes the imperial figure of Napoleon. At the very foot of the crumbling rampart, a symbol of the fall of defeated Girona, a bay tree flourishes, a sign of the city's moral victory.

Modest Urgell
i Inglada (1839-1919)
THE RAMPARTS AROUND GIRONA

c. 1871
Oil on canvas
67.7 x 116.5 cm
Girona Provincial Council
Art Collection. Reg.
no. 250.295

FLOOR 4
Room 17

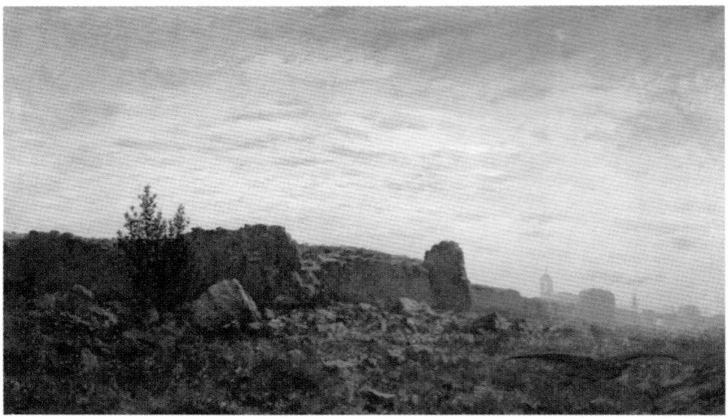

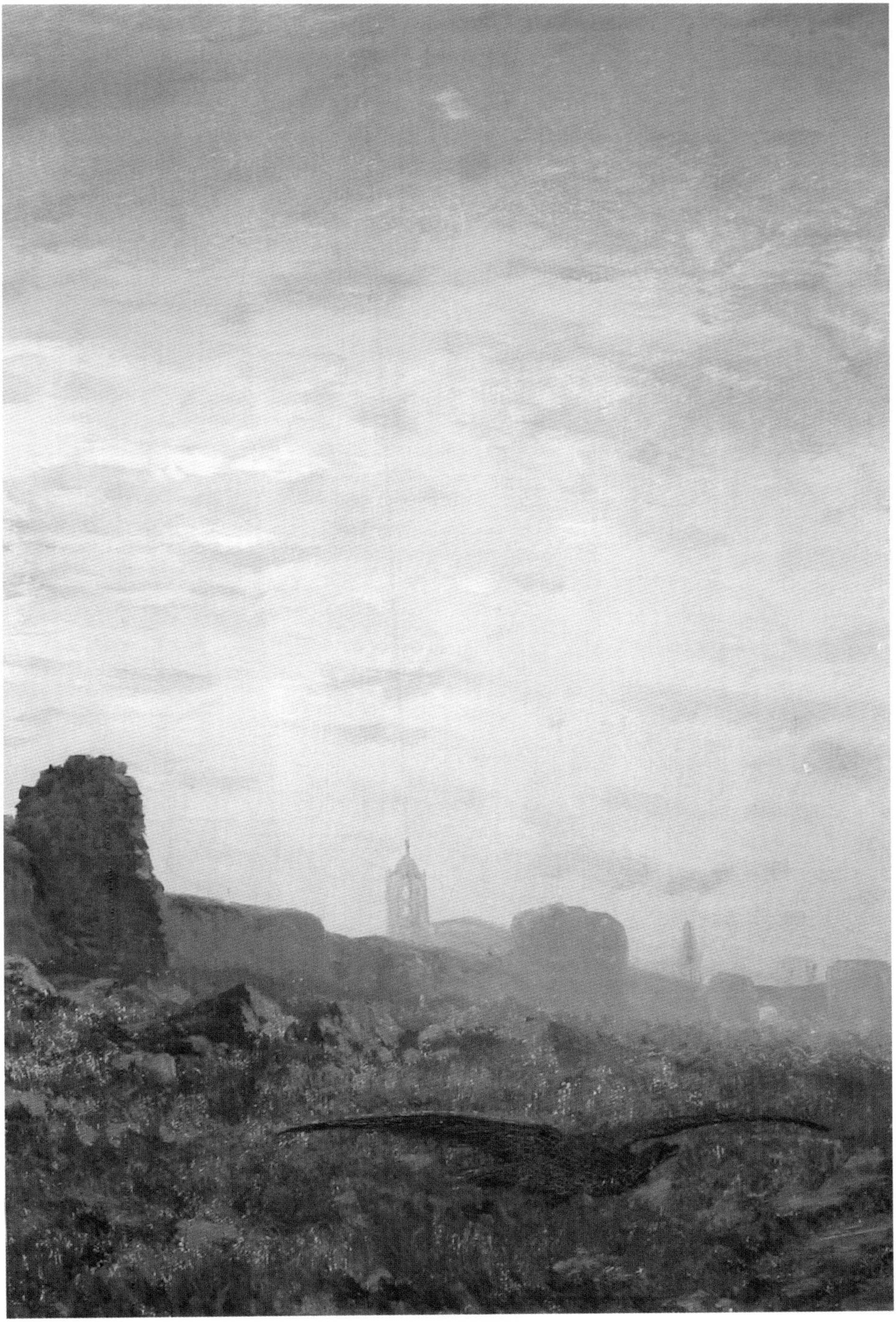

17. A GREEN AND BLUE LANDSCAPE

The flock, guarded by the shepherd, grazes under the bare branches of three trees in this oil painting typical of Joaquim Vayreda, fully expressive of his world and very representative of the Olot school, a phenomenon of outstanding importance in the history of Catalan art for its status as a focus of pictorial creation outside Barcelona. Born in Girona and trained at the School of Fine Arts in Olot, Vayreda soon grew tired of the routine lessons he received and went to Barcelona, where he met up with Ramon Martí i Alsina, and then to Paris, where he became acquainted with the work of Camille Corot and the Barbizon school, the inspiration for the vague Impressionism that permeates his paintings, which were initially poorly received and finally acclaimed by the public. This **landscape**, which finds the best reflection of the serene peace of the Garrotxa region in the balance of blues and greens, goes beyond the academicist rhetoric of the time to open up new irreversible paths of artistic renewal.

Joaquim Vayreda i Vila
(1843-1894)
FLOCK OF SHEEP
IN A FIELD

1881
Oil on canvas
78 x 120 cm
Girona Provincial Council
Art Collection. Reg.
no. 250.292

FLOOR 4
Room 17

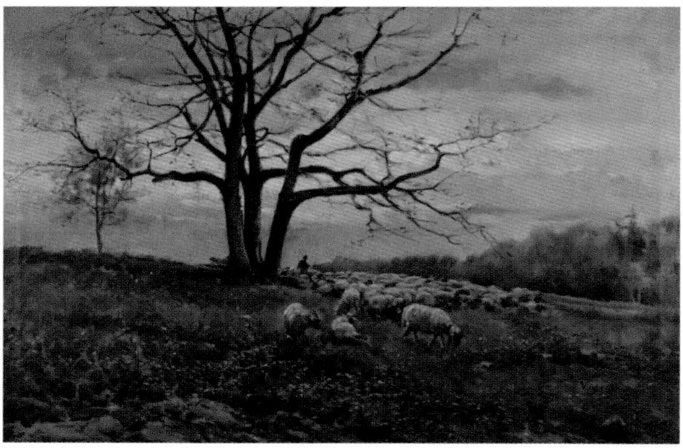

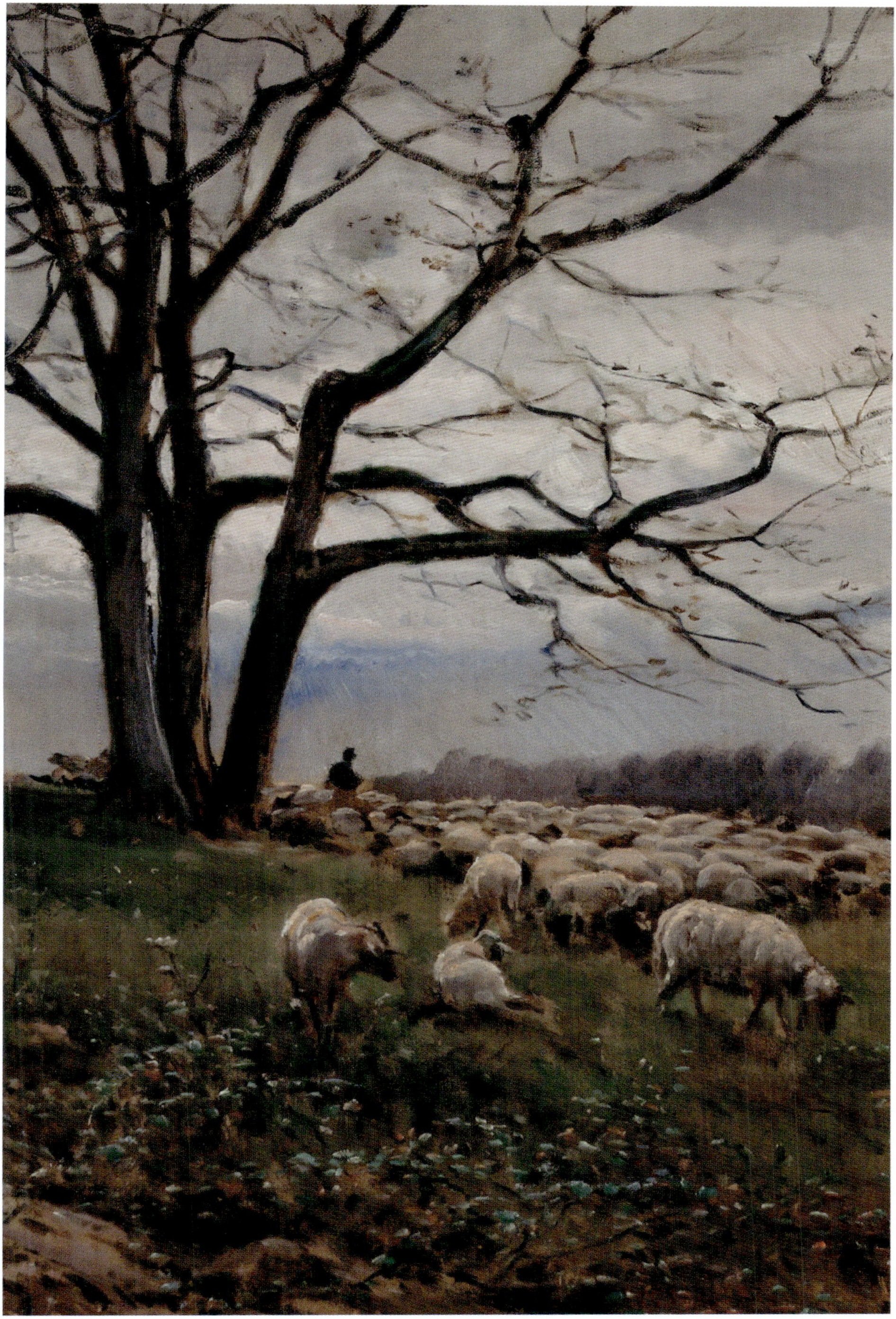

18. HISTORY AGAINST THE LIGHT

When he was already a famous writer and painter, Santiago Rusiñol visited Girona and fell in love with it, to the point of staying in the city for long periods in summer and autumn every year. On many days, having eaten and taken a nap, he made his way to Sant Daniel Valley to the Can Fontan hostel, which was one of his favourite refuges. He painted this **canvas**, conceived as a synthesis of the old city, from the first bend on that road. Its three main monuments – Girona Cathedral, Sant Feliu and Sant Pere – are cut out against the golden sky of the sunset, and the city wall rises on a soft green that descends from the heroic stones to the modest vegetation of the vegetable gardens. The whole scene is imbued with the light of dusk, when shapes become softer and colours are sweeter. Beyond its objective approach, the painting has a strong subjective character; beyond the realistic detail, we can sense the desire to capture the great defining features of the spirit of Girona.

Santiago Rusiñol i Prats
(1861-1931)
GIRONA

c. 1915
Oil on canvas
93 x 123 cm
Girona Provincial Council
Art Collection. Reg.
no. 250.279

FLOOR 4
Room 17

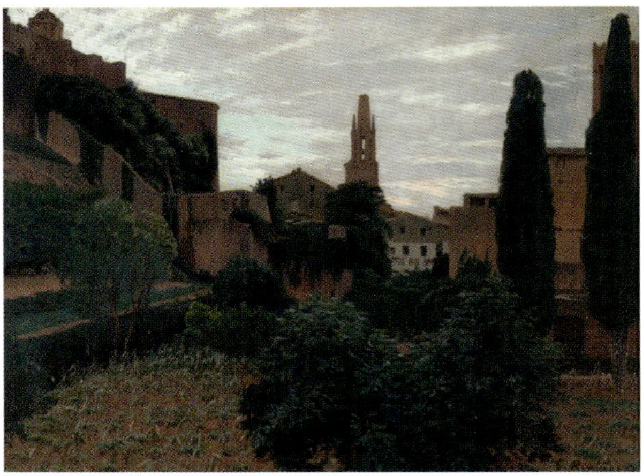

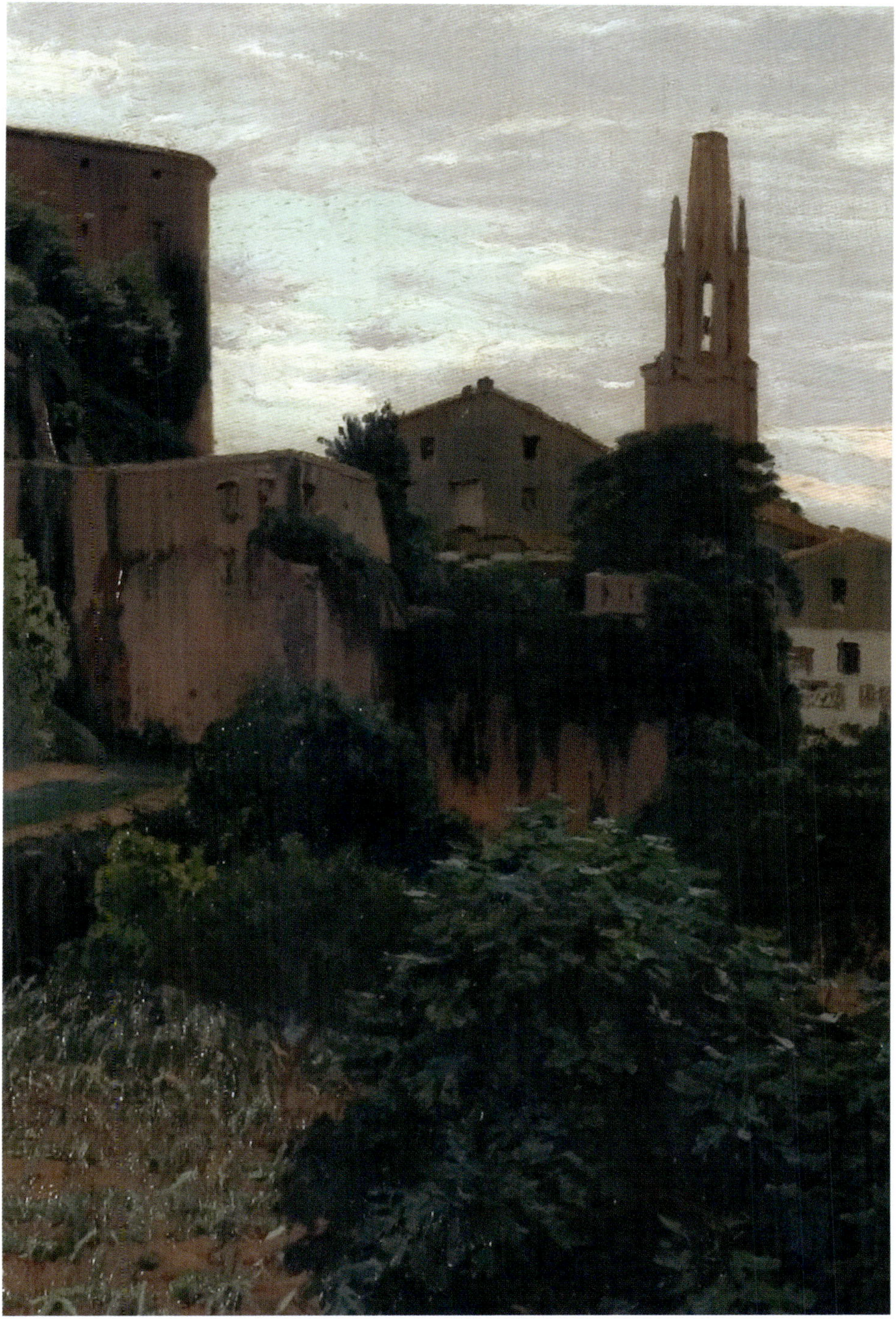

19. FROM ANECDOTE TO SYMBOL

When Olot-born Miquel Blay, one of the leading lights of Catalan art nouveau, sculpted this figure, he was only twenty-five years old and was studying in Paris, for the third year in a row, on a scholarship from Girona Provincial Council. Blay wanted to honour the people of Girona who fought heroically in the Napoleonic sieges of 1808-1809 and symbolised them in this brave young man, inspired by Gian Lorenzo Bernini's *David*, wielding his spear against invisible enemies. The Girona historian Carles Rahola, in a piece written in 1938, in the midst of the Spanish Civil War, said that, through the magic of art, this **statue** surpassed the specific historical anecdote to reach a permanent and symbolic value and portray "the citizen of Girona, the Catalan, standing against that and all invasions." For this and other writings, Rahola was found guilty of the crime of military rebellion: Franco's army sentenced him to death in a drumhead court-martial and shot him in Girona in 1939.

Miquel Blay i Fàbrega (1866-1936)
AGAINST THE INVADER

1891
Plaster
165 x 74.3 x 90 cm
Girona Provincial Council Art Collection. Reg. no. 26.550

FLOOR 4
Room 17

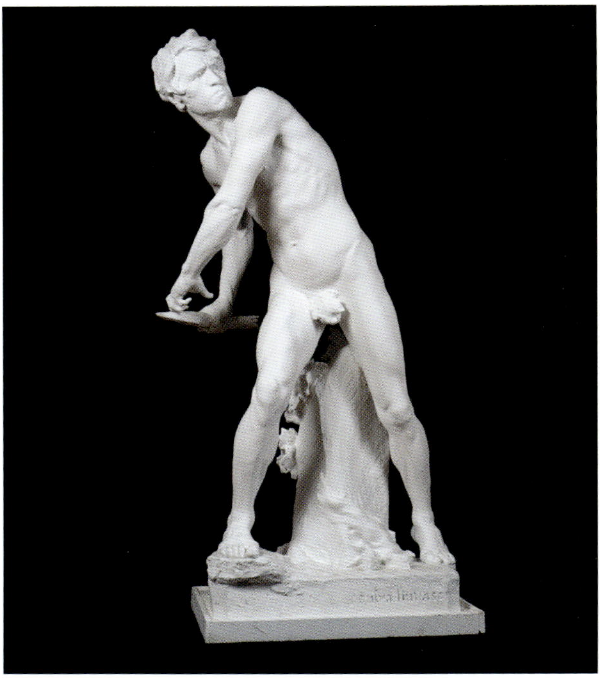

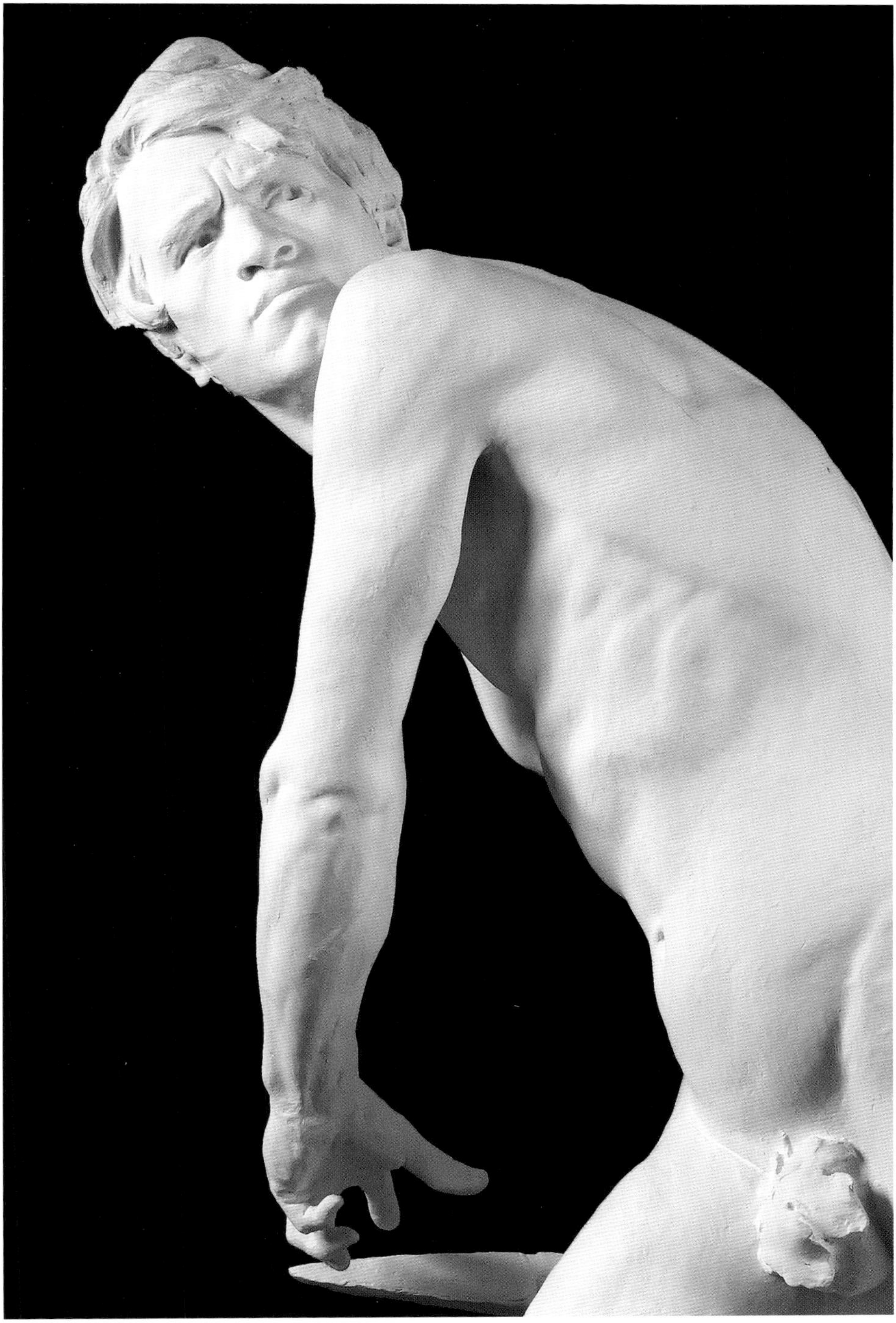

20. THE HEAD OF A NOVELIST

Girona-born Ricard Guinó is famous as the actual maker of many of the sculptural works of the Impressionist painter Pierre-Auguste Renoir, unable to sculpt them himself due to progressive rheumatism. Guinó made this **bust** of the writer and painter Prudenci Bertrana when he was not yet twenty years old. Shortly afterwards, in 1910, it was Bertrana who introduced the young sculptor to Aristides Maillol, who was passing through Girona. Excited, Maillol took him to Paris as an assistant. There, Guinó collaborated with Maurice Denis and worked for Renoir until the master's death, without abandoning a career that would put him among the best official sculptors in France. Bertrana's daughter, Aurora, offered this bust of her father to Girona in 1971 to be placed in the Public Library. The Provincial Council of the time rejected it, but instead the City Council commissioned a replica and placed it in Plaça de Catalunya, in a monument to the novelist who has best described the city.

Ricard Guinó i Boix
(1890-1973)
BUST OF PRUDENCI BERTRANA

c. 1923
Lacquered plaster
45 x 42 x 29 cm
Girona Provincial Council Art Collection. Reg. no. 131.231

FLOOR 4
Room 18

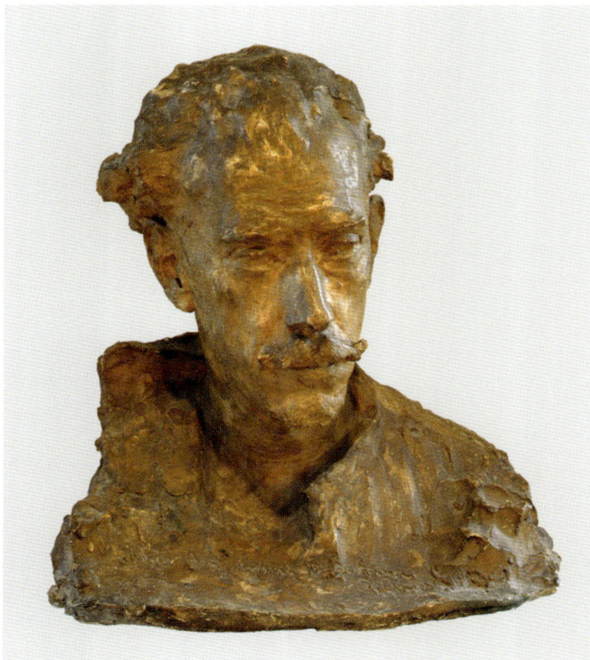

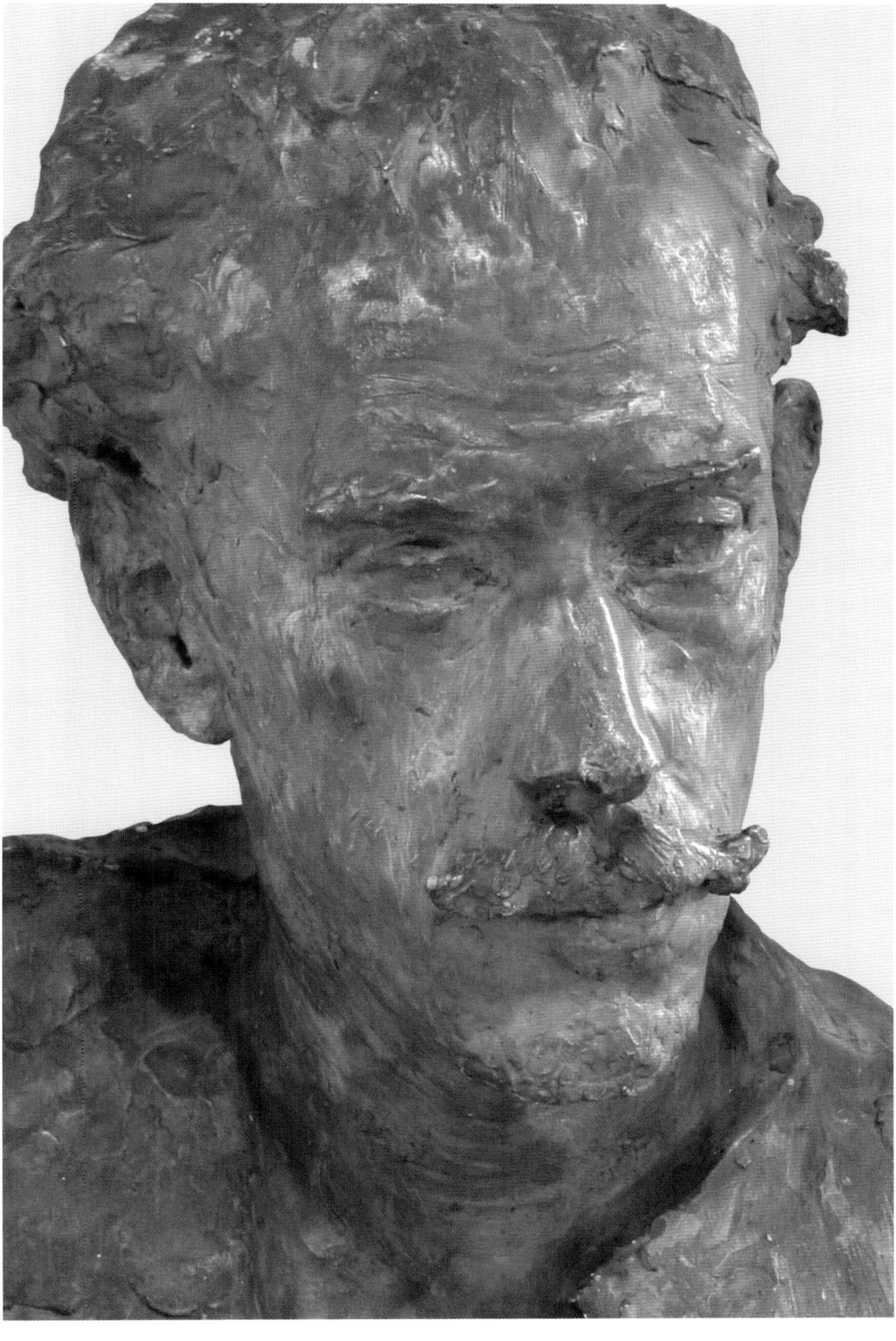

21. FULL MOON OVER THE RIVER

The houses on the Onyar River are the view most reproduced by painters in Girona. Although everyone portrays them in broad daylight, the artist and writer Prudenci Bertrana did so at night in this **oil painting** that, in the guise of a conventional piece, conceals all the mystery of the art nouveau city, of which he was one of its greatest exponents. The full moon, which had already dominated the verses of the Romantics, permeated the lyrical visions of the twilight and decadent Girona of the early twentieth century. This pictorial vision, full of melancholy, has a literary counterpoint in a fragment of the novel *El vagabund*, written by Bertrana fifteen years later, when the prestige acquired as a writer had already eclipsed his initial fame as a painter. The main character of that story, who is an *alter ego* of the author, contemplates the night perspective of the city with "the ramshackle and picturesque row of old and uneven houses confusedly reflected in the thick calm water of the river."

Prudenci Bertrana i Compte (1867-1941)
FULL MOON AT GIRONA

c. 1913
Oil on canvas
69 x 55 cm
Girona Provincial Council Art Collection. Reg. no. 250.242

FLOOR 4
Room 18

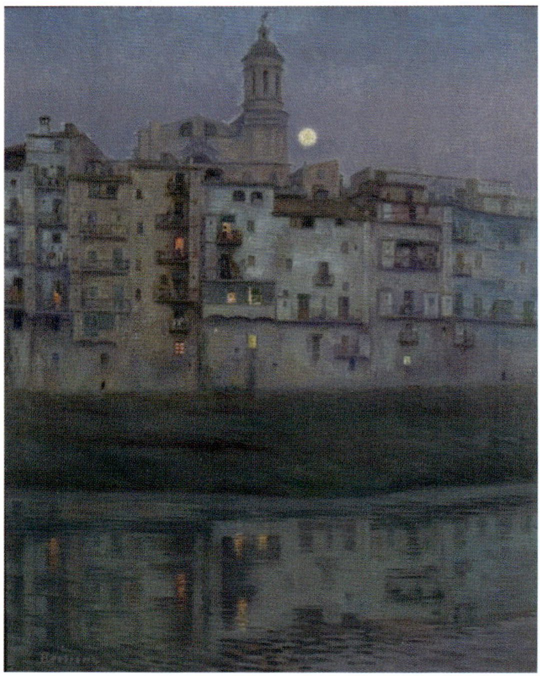

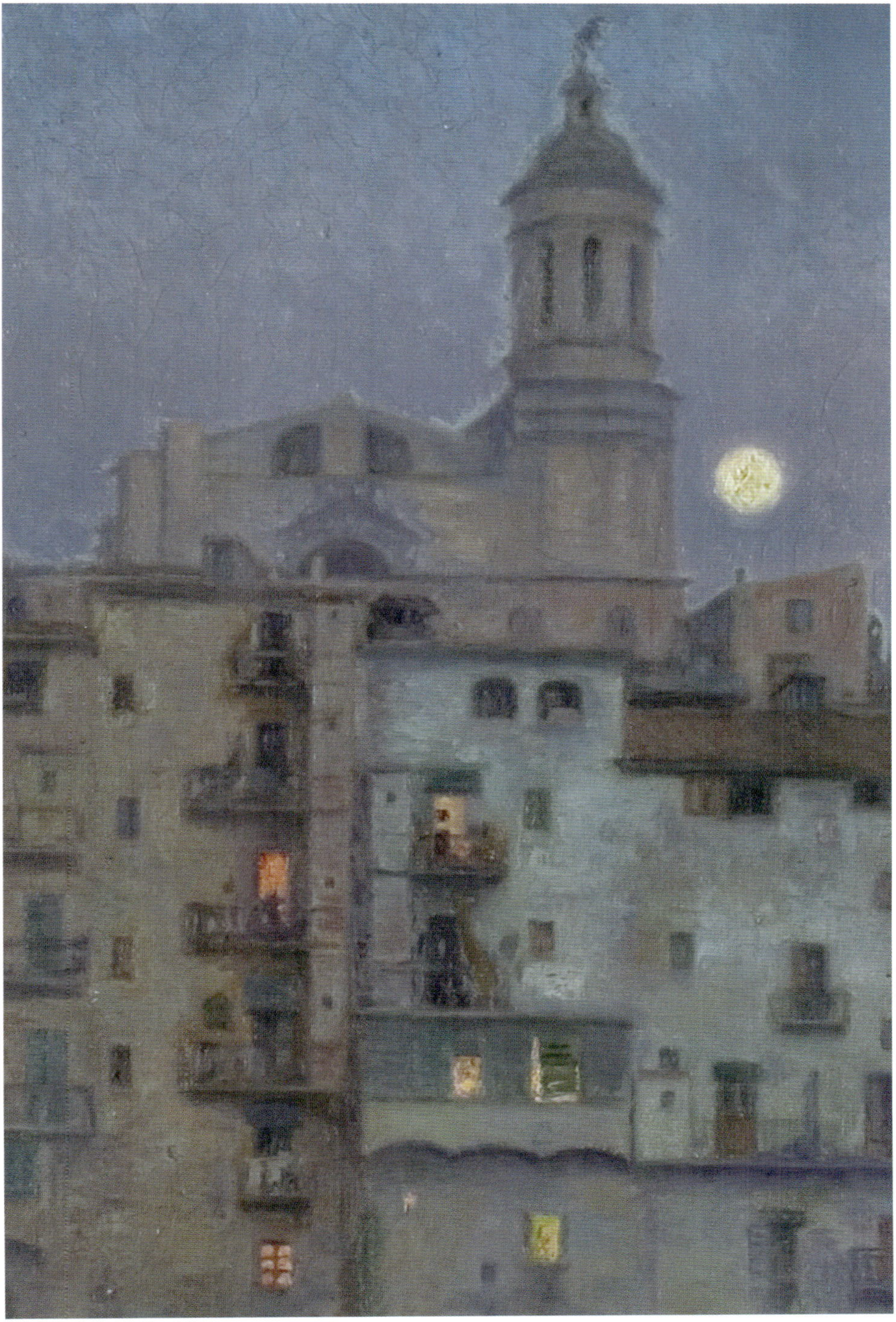

22. TRIPTYCH OF A DEAD AND LIVING CITY

Born in Warsaw, Maria Melania Klingsland took the artistic name Mela Muter, derived from the surname of her husband, Mutermilch. She arrived in Catalonia in 1911, from Paris, and stayed in Girona until the outbreak of the First World War, in 1914, the date of this unique **oil painting**, unusual for its conception and expressionist style, both harsh and lyrical. Mela Muter, according to her own confession, "tried to reproduce the whole city in the triptych formed by the two large trees in the foreground." It is, therefore, both a realistic portrait and a symbolic vision of early twentieth century Girona: a city that seemed dead, but that was very much alive inside. While the old houses and the lazy river show it drowsy and secluded, the golden façade of the cathedral, which rises timidly in the background, framed by the two trunks that make it resemble a triptych, embodies the vitality that emerges above the apparent death and reveals the secret of the Girona paradox.

Mela (Maria Melania) Mutermilch (1876-1967)
THE ONYAR RIVER IN GIRONA
[*By the River Ban*]

1914
Oil on canvas
100 x 100 cm
Girona Provincial Council Art Collection. Reg. no. 250.336

FLOOR 4
Room 18

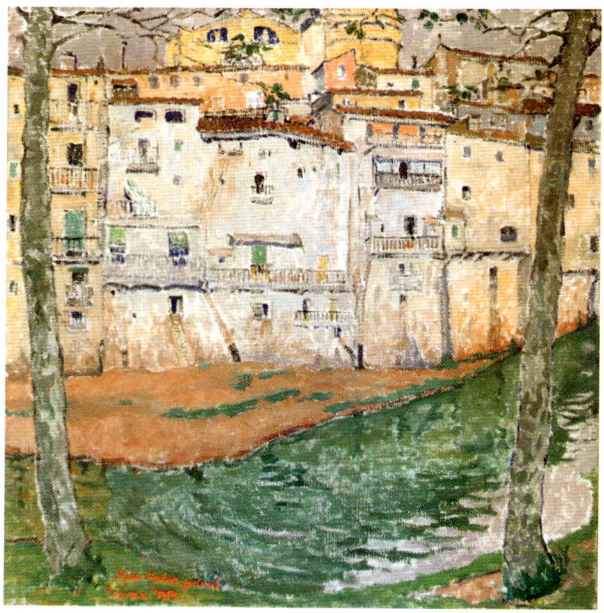

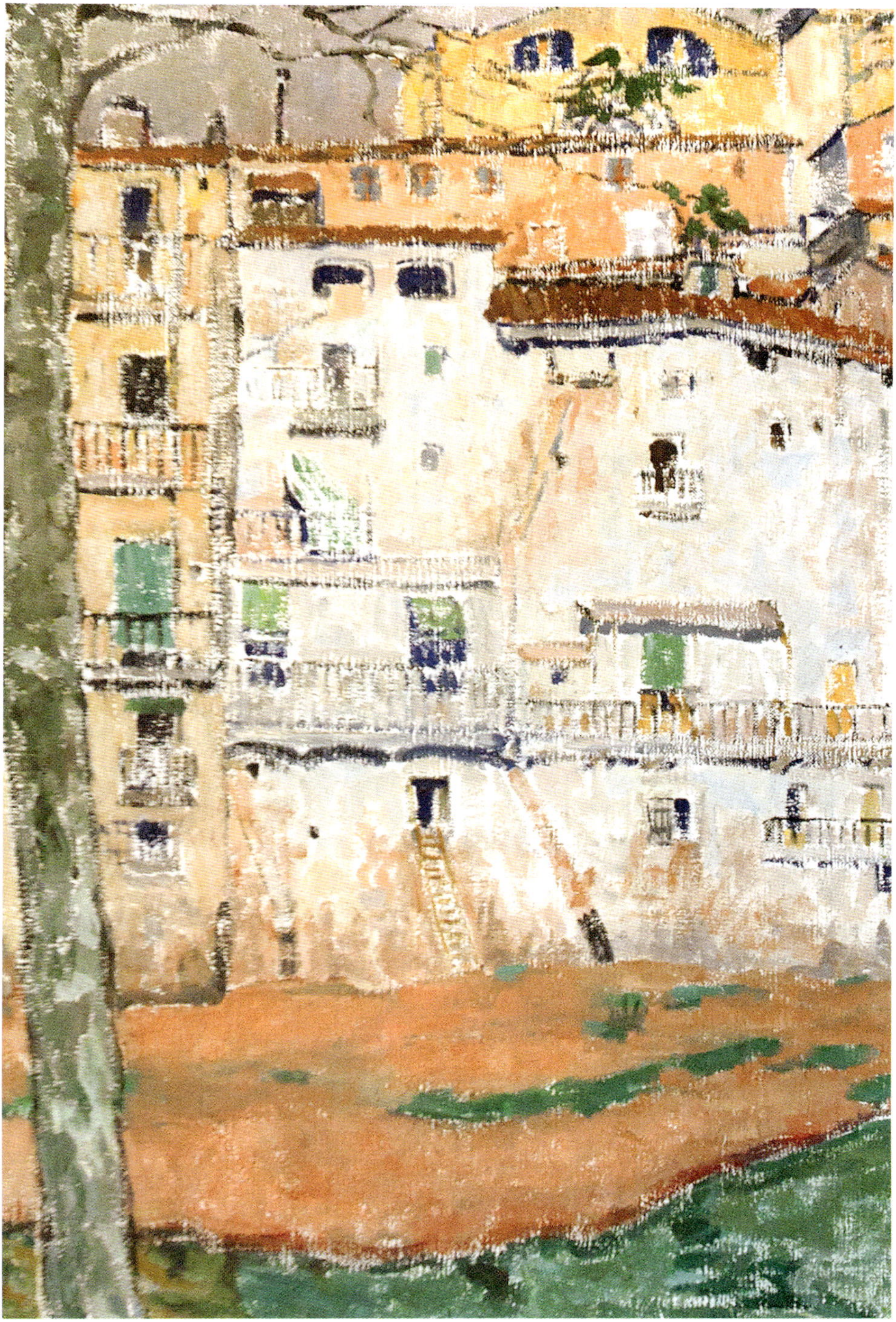

23. STAIRWAY OF AN UNMOVING TIME

Josep Aguilera, born in Salt (Gironès), opened a drawing academy in Girona and became a teacher and director of the city's Municipal School of Fine Arts. After the Spanish Civil War he moved permanently to Barcelona, where he died in 1955. He did not belong to any definite school but was able to create his own style, which makes his works immediately identifiable. With masses of chiaroscuro and evanescent forms, he always painted the same sleeping city, anchored in an unmoving time. The landscapes without edges, the volumes muffled by the light and the silhouettes stylised by the mist were the product of his emotion, but also the expression of his mood, constantly depressed by the difficulties of a precarious existence. In this charcoal **drawing**, a hooded woman accompanies a girl to the church of Sant Martí; the trembling silhouettes are swallowed up by the immensity of one of the most prodigious scenes in old Girona.

Josep Aguilera i Martí (1882-1955)
STAIRWAY TO SANT MARTÍ

1936
Charcoal and pastel on paper
71 x 77 cm
Girona Provincial Council Art Collection. Reg. no. 130.767

FLOOR 4
Room 18

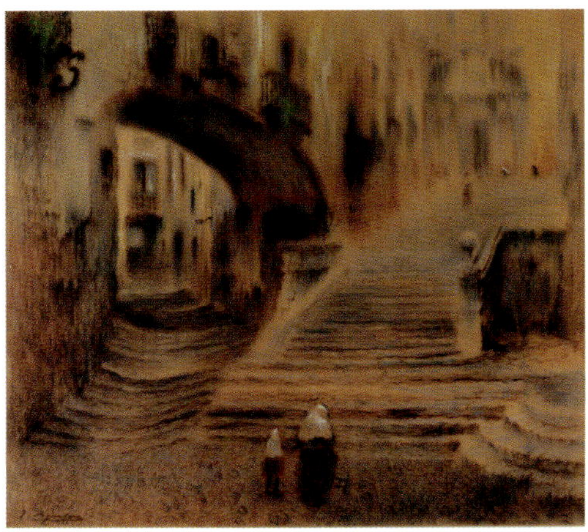

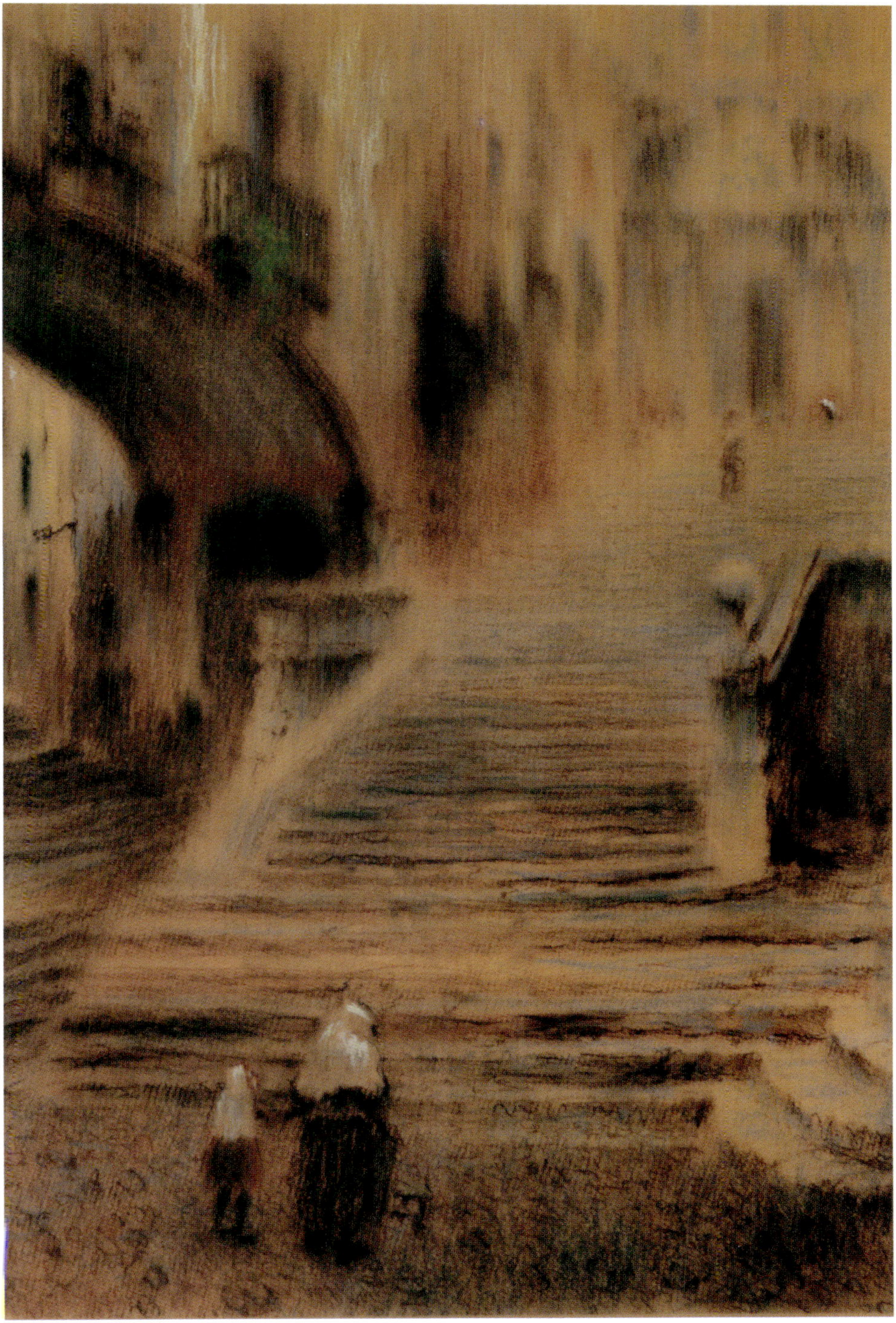

24. A SCULPTURE ON PAPER

Fidel Aguilar, born in Girona, had a short dark life. Death betrayed him when he was not yet twenty-three years old, but with enough time to have established an original and exclusive sculptural work. Art historians place this completely self-taught artist alongside the great *Noucentisme* sculptors, such as Casanovas, Clarà and Rebull, and say that, if he had lived, he could have become as important as Brancusi with his conciseness, supreme stylisation and the rhythmic strength of his oeuvre. This woman's head, drawn with masses rather than with lines, in which the strokes foreshadow the volumes, seems to await the enduring glory of marble, the definitive embodiment of the sculptor's dream. It is a **face** that is at once palpable and intangible, sensual and mystical, temporary and eternal, illuminated with an ephemeral burst and closed in on itself like the style of its creator, his life unjustly truncated by premature death.

Fidel Aguilar i Marcó
(1894-1917)
HEAD OF A WOMAN

c. 1916
Charcoal on paper
35 x 27 cm
Girona Provincial Council
Art Collection. Reg.
no. 250.235

FLOOR 4
Room 18

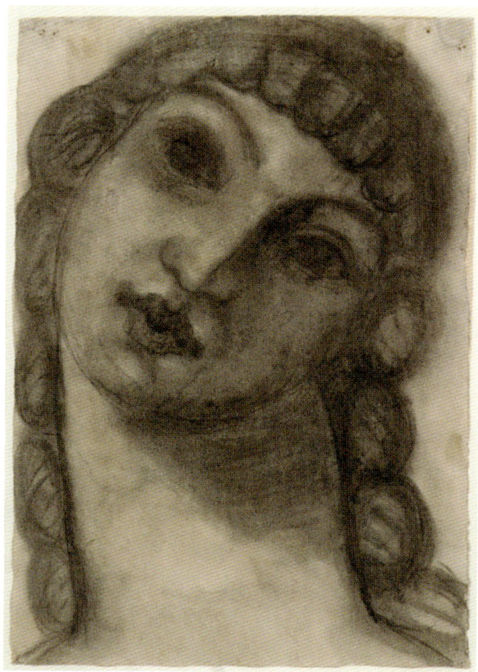

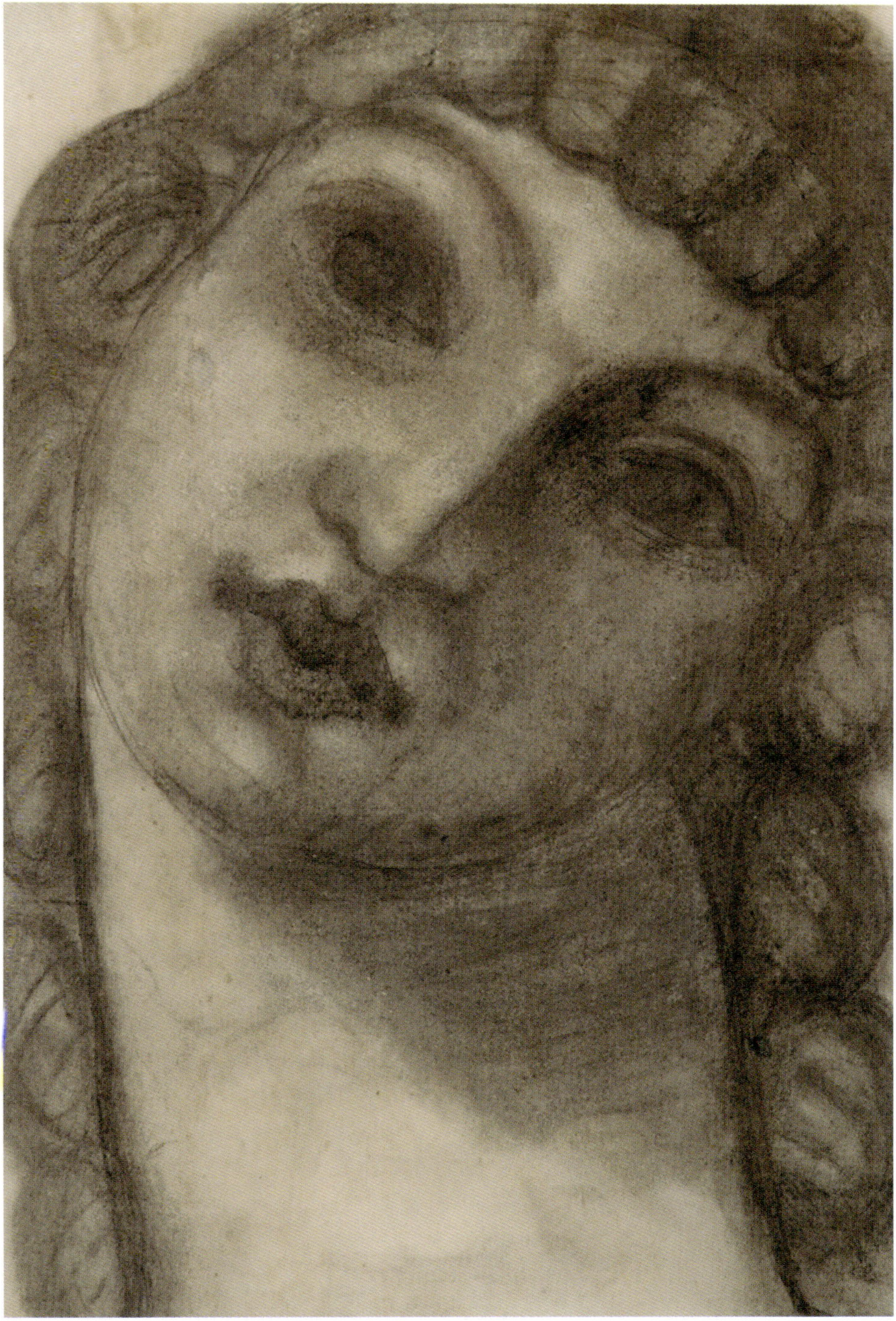

Girona
Art Museum
Floor plan

GIRONA ART MUSEUM

- Romanesque
- Gothic
- 16th century
- 17th - 18th centuries
- 19th century
- 20th century
- Temporary rooms:
  GF. Area 1
  F2. Area 3, L'Espai
  F4. Prison
  F5. Area 2
- Monographic rooms
- Discovery point

GROUND FLOOR

Entrance

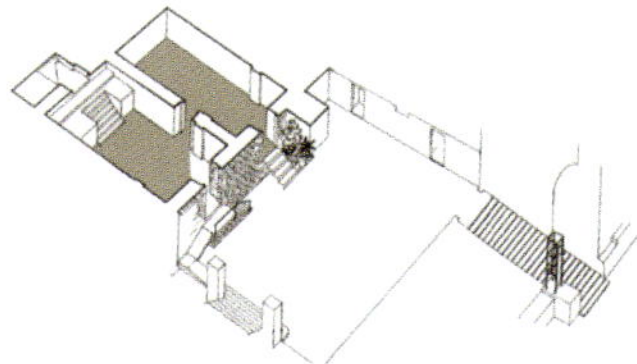

FLOOR 1

1. Fragment of an early Christian gravestone
2. Portable altar of Sant Pere de Rodes
3. Cruïlles beam
4. *Bede's Book of Homilies*
5. Apse of Pedrinyà
6. *The Lioness*
7. *Our Lady of Hope*
8. *Calvary*
9. *Usuard's Martyrology*
10. Altarpiece of Sant Miquel de Cruïlles
11. Altarpiece of Sant Pere de Púbol
12. *Preaching of Saint Felix in Girona*

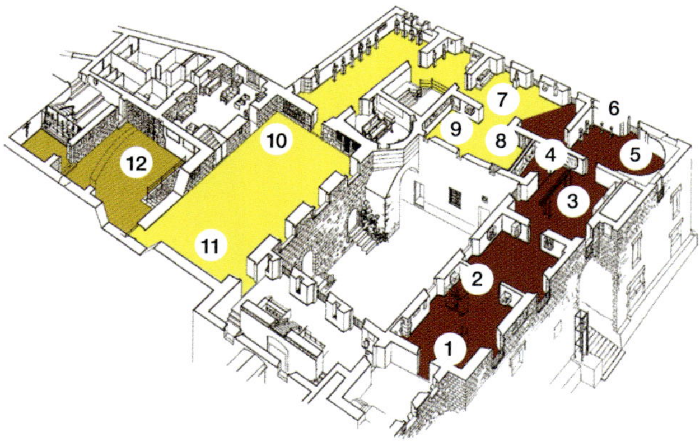

FLOOR 2

13. Glassmaker's work tables
14. The *Creation* panel

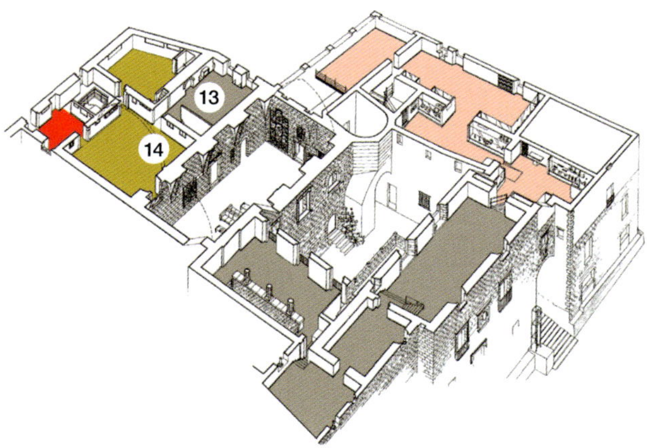

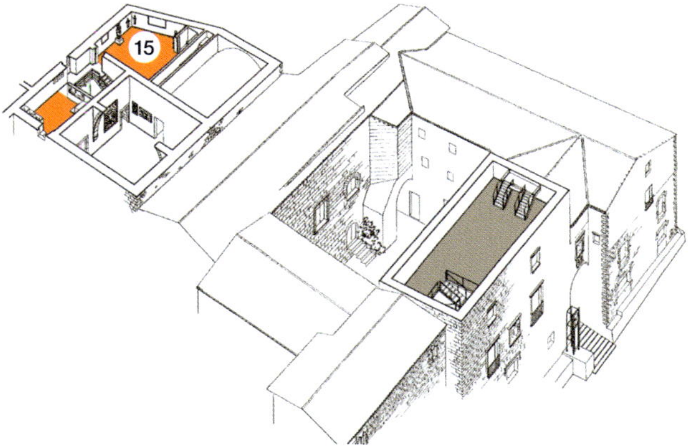

FLOOR 3

15. *Marriage of the Virgin Mary*

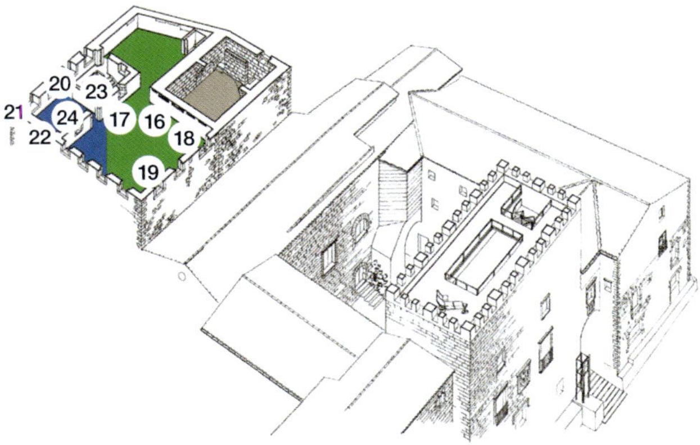

FLOOR 4

16. *The Ramparts Around Girona*
17. *Flock of Sheep in a Field*
18. *Girona*
19. *Against the Invader*
20. *Bust of Prudenci Bertrana*
21. *Full Moon at Girona*
22. *The Onyar River in Girona [By the River Bank]*
23. *Stairway to Sant Martí*
24. *Head of a Woman*

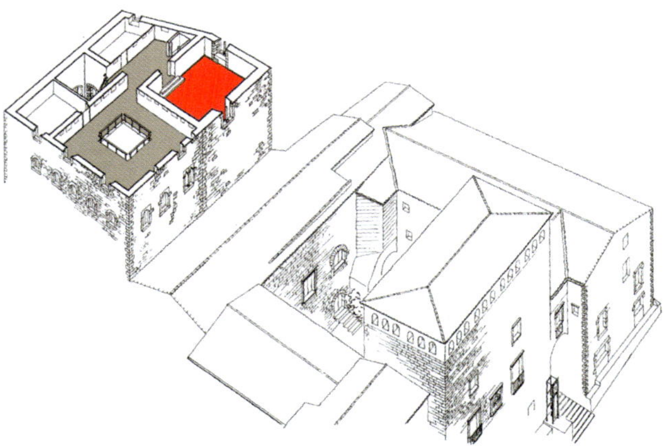

FLOOR 5

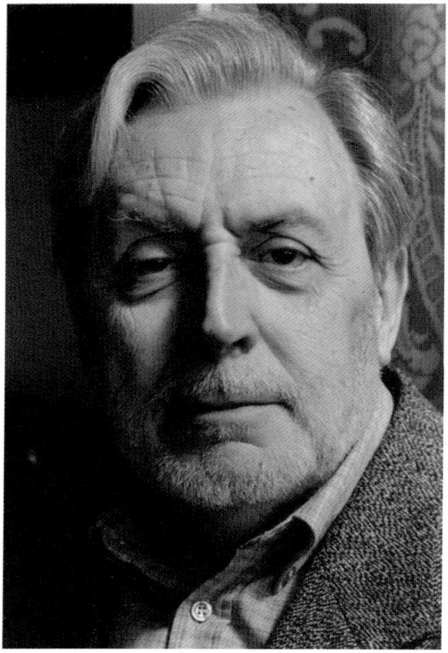

Narcís-Jordi Aragó i Masó
(Girona, 1932-2016)
Lawyer, journalist, writer and art critic

Narcís-Jordi Aragó enjoyed a long and full career as a journalist. Co-founder of the Girona Journalists Association (1977) and the Catalan Journalists Association (1985), he worked for Ràdio Girona, where he presented several programmes, and was editor-in-chief of the magazine *Vida Catòlica* (1962-1967), editor of the weekly *Presència* (1967-1980) and *Revista de Girona* (1985), as well as correspondent for *Tele/eXpres* (1970-1980). From 1979 he contributed to the newspaper *El Punt*, and in 2007 he chaired its editorial board. He was also director of the Information and Documentation Centre of the Girona Chamber of Commerce and Industry (1975-1995).

He produced an extensive amount of historical and literary writing about Girona, his city of birth and residence, becoming its distinguished guide and chronicler. *Girona grisa i negra* (1972, co-authored), *La Devesa, paradís perdut* (1980), *Girona ara i sempre* (1982), *Guia de la Girona monumental* and *L'Empordà d'anar i tornar* (1992) are some of his best-known works, along with numerous joint publications.

Corresponding member of the Sant Jordi Royal Academy of Fine Arts (1987), he received several awards, such as the Honorary Prize for Communications awarded by Barcelona Provincial Council (2000), the "Ciutadania" distinction from Girona City Council (2001) and the Cultural Merit Distinction from the Faculty of Humanities at Girona University (2007). In 2002 he was given the Creu de Sant Jordi of the Government of Catalonia.

Linked to the Museu d'Art (Md'A) in Girona since its establishment in 1976, he chaired the Museum's Friends Association between 1996 and 1999. He wrote extensively for this institution, including this guide to a selection of *24 Key Pieces of the Md'A* (2003), a visit to the rooms of the Museum through his perspective and prose, which, seventeen years later, we are republishing.

Girona is also indebted to him for the donation of the Masó legacy: the *Noucentista*-style house overlooking the Onyar River (today a house-museum) and the documentary archive of his uncle, the architect Rafael Masó. A legacy managed by the Fundació Rafael Masó in Girona, of which he was honorary president until his death.

GIRONA ART MUSEUM

Management
Carme Clusellas

Technical team
Elena Boix, Aurèlia Carbonell,
Carme Martinell, Antoni Monturiol

Administrative staff
Adriana Cle, Dori Mesa

Conservation
Josep Clusells

Reception staff
Teresa Herms, Pilar Ramírez,
Mar Ribot, Pere Romans

Girona Art Museum
Pujada de la Catedral, 12
17004 Girona
Tel. +34 972 20 38 34 / +34 972 20 95 36
Fax +34 972 22 75 95
www.museuart.cat

md'A Museu d'Art de Girona

Generalitat de Catalunya
Departament de Cultura

Bisbat de Girona

Diputació de Girona

CATALOGUE

Published by
Girona Art Museum
(Catalan Agency for Cultural Heritage)

Editing
Carme Clusellas

Coordination
Aurèlia Carbonell
Àngels Miralles

Technical support
Carme Martinell
Antoni Monturiol

Author of the texts
Narcís-Jordi Aragó

Linguistic advice and translations
Traduccions LINK

Photographs by
Girona City Council. CRDI (Josep Maria Oliveras)
© Catalan Centre for the Restoration of Moveable Property
(CRBMC)
Rafel Bosch
Rafael López-Monné

Printing
Nexe Impressions

Graphic design
La Fonda Gràfica

Cover image
Lluís Borrassà, altarpiece of Sant Miquel de Cruïlles (detail) (c. 1416). Girona Art Museum.
Reg. no. MDG 29. Diocese of Girona Collection

24 KEY PIECES OF THE GIRONA ART MUSEUM,
2020. LD: GI 1406-2020
ISBN 978-84-18601-19-4

This publication is a revision and updating
of the first edition of 2003.

BIBLIOTECA DE CATALUNYA - DADES CIP

Museu d'Art (Girona, Catalunya), autor
[24 obres clau del MD'A]

24 obres clau del Museu d'Art de Girona
Reedició de l'obra 24 obres clau del MD'A, publicada l'any 2003
ISBN 9788418601194
I. Aragó, Narcís-Jordi, 1932-2016, escriptor d'un comentari afegit II. Títol
III. Títol: Vint-i-quatre obres clau del Museu d'Art de Girona
1. Museu d'Art (Girona, Catalunya) – Guies
069.02:7(460.233)(036)